Reducing Gun Deaths and Injuries

A Social Marketing Approach

By

Nancy R. Lee

Reducing Gun Deaths and Injuries: A Social Marketing Approach

By Nancy R. Lee

This book first published 2023

Ethics International Press Ltd, UK

British Library Cataloguing in Publication Data

A catalogue record for this book is available from the British Library

Print Book ISBN: 978-1-80441-094-3

eBook ISBN: 978-1-80441-095-0

Table of Contents

Foreword ix

Prologue.. xi

About the Author xii

1. *The Facts* - To Inform and Inspire.. 1

2. *A Social Marketing Approach* - Behavior Change
for Good 19

3. *Gun Owners* - Storing Guns Safely to Reduce Youth/
Children Gun Suicides.. 29

4. *Friends* - Reaching Out to Someone Who Seems Suicidal........ 39

5. *Medical Providers* -Helping to Reduce Youth
Gun Suicides 50

6. *Upstanders* - "Say Something" to Report
Warning Signs of a School Shooting... 60

7. *School Threat Assessment Teams* – Identifying
& Intervening With Potential Shooters... 71

8. *Heroic Bystanders* -Becoming First Responders........................ 81

9. *Public Event Attendees* - Having an Exit Plan 92

10. *Communities* - Reducing Youth Handgun Carrying............. 101

11. *Gang Members* - Participating in Group Meetings 110

12. *Neighbors* - Greening Abandoned Vacant Lots 123

13. *Communities* - Enhancing Street Lighting 133

14. *Street Outreach Workers* - Mediating Conflicts
& Preventing Retaliatory Violence 144

15. *Citizens* - Advocating for Change 155

16. *Potential Victims of Domestic Violence Homicides* -
Getting Help from Mobile Apps 167

17. *Citizens Who See Something Suspicious* - Say Something 178

18. *Social Media Groups* - Mitigating Potential
Gun Violence 189

19. *Local Governmental Agencies* - Distributing
Free Gun Locking Devices 200

20. *Governmental Agencies* - Offering Monetary
Incentives for Safe Firearm Storage 210

21. *News Reporters & Journalists* - Increasing Public
Concern & Inspiring Action 218

22. *Employers* - Providing Workplace Safety Programs 229

23. *Highlights of Case Examples In This Book* -
Facts, Audiences, Behaviors, Interventions, Applicable
Theories & Principles 239

Foreword

Of all the issues facing America today, one of the most consequential centers on gun violence. As the number of deaths continues to climb, the debate on how to make a meaningful reduction in such violence intensifies. Communities, neighborhoods, and families are torn apart. We hear the cry for justice and the call to end such violence. "Enough is enough" has become the common refrain.

What can we do? To whom can people turn? What resources are available? Such questions have traditionally been answered with a focus on increasing police officer presence in the problem areas, or enhancing penalties for those who perpetrate such crimes. Despite the additional officers and /or enhanced sentencing, the tragedies continue, and the discussions intensify. We see people circle the wagons around their political ideology related to the Second Amendment, resulting in little, if any, meaningful progress being made.

Rather than getting bogged down on the legal arguments on the right to bear arms, what if I told you there exists a resource that every community could benefit from? A resource that takes a holistic approach to the goal of reducing gun violence. What if I told you that such a resource is found in the pages of this book written by a Social Marketing expert, and that this expert really knows what she's talking about? What if I told you that this expert has experience working closely with a local police department to reduce crime, and that her work has made a positive difference in the community? Would you be interested in learning more? My hope is that your answer would be a resounding yes!

I have been a police officer for close to 30 years, serving as the Chief for most of those years. I have known social marketing expert and author Nancy Lee for many years through our local service club. Several years ago, she worked with my staff to identify ways to reduce crime in our neighborhoods. She analyzed our data, identified a solution, and helped us market our *Lock It or Lose It* campaign. With her help she made our community safer. She has now taken her passion for public safety to focus on reducing gun violence. In this, her latest book, *Reducing Gun Deaths & Injuries: A Social Marketing Approach,* she shares 20 efforts communities can take to make meaningful changes to reduce gun violence. I am very pleased to know that Nancy's work is now available to everyone, and I am equally pleased to know that she can once again help to make our communities safer.

Ed Holmes, Chief of Police

Mercer Island, Washington

Prologue

It was on Tuesday, May 24, 2022, the day of the mass school shooting at Robb Elementary School in Uvalde, Texas, that I decided to author this book. I not only heard that 19 children and two teachers were killed during the shooting, I also read that the shooter had sent text messages to a friend sharing that "Ima go shoot up a elementary school rn (right now)."[1] I later learned from the Sandy Hook Promise Foundation website that *"93% of school shooters planned the attack in advance"*[2], and that *"in 4 out of 5 school shootings, at least one other person had knowledge of the attacker's plan but failed to report it."*[3] And then I read that almost *half of school shooters stole the gun from a family member.*[4]

It was clear to me that **Social Marketing,** a proven discipline for influencing *Behavior Change for Good,* is applicable for reducing deaths such as these, with data and research inspiring areas of focus, priority audiences, desired behaviors, audience insights and the 20 program *intervention strategies* discussed in this book.

Nancy R. Lee

---

[1] The Guardian, "Texas gunman allegedly texted German teenager plans for attack" (May 2022), accessed at https://www.theguardian.com/us-news/2022/may/26/texas-shooter-texted-german-teenager-plans

[2] Sandy Hook Promise, " Say Something Creates Cultural Change That Leads To Safer Schools" (2022), accessed September 28, 2022, https://www.sandyhookpromise.org/our-programs/say-something/

[3] Sandy Hook Promise, "17 Facts About Gun Violence And School shootings" (2023), accessed at https://www.sandyhookpromise.org/our-programs/say-something/

[4] BROOKINGS, "School shootings: What we know about them, and what we can do to prevent them" (January 2022), R. Kowalski, accessed at https://www.brookings.edu/blog/brown-center-chalkboard/2022/01/26/school-shootings-what-we-know-about-them-and-what-we-can-do-to-prevent-them/

About the Author

Nancy Lee has more than 30 years of professional marketing experience, with special expertise in Social Marketing, the proven discipline for *Behavior Change for Social Good.*

She is president of Social Marketing Services, Inc., in Seattle, Washington, a strategic advisor for social marketing campaigns at C+C, a communications firm in Seattle, and an Affiliate Instructor at the University of Washington where she teaches social marketing in the Public Administration and Public Health programs. She also teaches an online Professional Certificate Course for the International Social Marketing Association. With more than 30 years of practical marketing experience in the public and private sectors, Ms. Lee has held numerous corporate marketing positions, including Vice President and Director of Marketing for Rainier

Bank, Washington State's second-largest bank, and Director of Marketing for Seattle Children's Hospital.

She has consulted with more than 100 nonprofit organizations and has participated in the development of more than 200 social marketing campaign strategies for public sector agencies. Clients in the public sector include the Centers for Disease Control and Prevention (CDC), Environmental Protection Agency (EPA), Washington State Department of Health, Office of Crime Victims Advocacy, Department of Ecology, Department of Fisheries and Wildlife, Office of Superintendent of Public Instruction, Washington Traffic Safety Commission, County Health and Transportation Departments, and the City of Seattle and City of Mercer Island.

She has co-authored 15 books on Social Marketing, 13 with Philip Kotler, and has contributed numerous articles to professional journals including the *Stanford Social Innovation Review, Social Marketing Quarterly, Journal of Social Marketing,* and *The Public Manager.*

She is a founder and past president of the Pacific Northwest Social Marketing Association (PNSMA), and serves on the Board of the International Social Marketing Association (iSMA), as well as the Social Marketing Association of North America. (SMANA).

Nancy R. Lee, MBA
President, Social Marketing Services, Inc.
Strategic Advisor, C+C
Affiliate Instructor, University of Washington

Chapter 1

The Facts
To Inform and Inspire

It was on Tuesday, May 24, 2022, the day of the mass school shooting at Robb Elementary School in Uvalde, Texas, that I decided to author this book. I not only heard that 19 children and two teachers were killed during the shooting, I also read that the shooter had sent text messages to a friend sharing that "Ima go shoot up a elementary school rn (right now)."[1] I later learned from the Sandy Hook Promise Foundation website that "93% of school shooters planned the attack in advance"[2], and that "in 4 out of 5 school shootings, at least one other person had knowledge of the attacker's plan but failed to report it."[3] And then I read that almost *half of school shooters stole the gun from a family member.*[4]

It was clear to me that **Social Marketing,** a proven discipline for influencing *Behavior Change for Good*, is applicable for reducing deaths such as these, with data and research inspiring areas of focus, priority audiences, desired behaviors, audience insights and *intervention strategies*.

Facts highlighted in this chapter related to gun deaths and injuries in the U.S. informed the selection of the 20 strategies outlined in this book to **influence voluntary behaviors to help reduce gun deaths and injuries,** and the selection of successful program efforts that highlight each approach. Major data points address the following key questions:

- What are *Basic Firearm Statistics* in the U.S. and how do we compare with other countries?
- What is known about *Gun Owners*?
- What is known about *Gun Shooters*?
- What is known about *Ownership of Guns That Were Used?*
- What is known About *Homicide Victims*?

Readers should note that most gun-related statistics noted throughout this book are those reported prior to 2020, given the unusual increases in violence and changes in circumstances due to the impact of the pandemic.

BASIC FIREARM STATISTICS IN THE U.S. & COMPARISONS TO OTHER COUNTRIES

How many people are injured and die from gun-related injuries every year?

- Nearly 40,000 Americans died from gun-related injuries every year from 2015 to 2019, an average of more than 100 *a day*.[5] And 200 more are shot and wounded a day.[6]
- On a per capita basis, there were 13.6 gun deaths per 100,000 people in 2020, the highest rate since the mid-1990s, but below a peak in 1974 of 16.3 gun deaths per 100,000 people.[7] Notably, the year 2020 saw the highest number of gun sales on record.[8]
- Gun injuries are the leading cause of death for children and teens since 2020 (Reported in 2023).[9]

What percentage of gun deaths are *Suicides*?

- The majority, more than 60%, of firearm deaths with intent each year are a result of suicides (2015 – 2019), with nearly 24,000 gun deaths from suicide in 2019.[10] That's more than 65 suicides on average every day.

- An estimated 90% of suicide attempts involving a gun ended in death.[11]

What percentage of gun deaths are *Homicides*?

- Homicide is most often described as the killing of a person by another with intent and does not include suicide. Homicides include different types of gun violence including *mass shootings* (e.g., at workplaces), *community violence* (e.g., street gangs, robberies), *domestic violence* and *police shootings*.[12]
- More than *a third (36%)* of gun shootings each year (2015-2019) are homicides.[13]
- An estimated 75% of all homicides are committed by firearm.[14]

How many homicides are *Mass Shootings*?

- Mass shootings are most often described as ones in which *four or more people are shot and killed*.[15]
- From 2015-2019, there were nearly *400 mass shooting incidents per year*, more than 1 a day on average. In 2020-2022, this number increased by more than 50% to more than 600 mass shootings per year.[16]

What percentage of gun deaths are categorized as *Legal Interventions*, ones primarily related to police-involved injuries or deaths?

- In 2019, CDC data indicated that less than 1% of gun deaths were due to legal interventions.[17]

How many *School Shootings* are there every year?

- For school years between 2015 and 2019 there were almost a total of 300 school shootings, with *more than 50, on average, each year, almost one a week*.[18]

- It is noted that *more than 80 school shootings* happened in the 2020-21 school year.[19]

Where do *School Shootings* happen most?

- States with the highest rates of school shootings per population (1970-2019) were the *District of Columbia, Alaska, and Louisiana*. States with the highest number of school shootings since 1970 are California, Texas, Florida, Michigan, Illinois.[20]
- States with the lowest rates of school shootings per population (1970-2019) were *New Jersey, Idaho, North Dakota, Maine, and West Virginia*. States with the lowest number of school shootings since 1970 are: North Dakota, Wyoming, Vermont, Maine, and Idaho.[21]
- Most common physical locations where school shootings happened in the 2020-21 school year were parking lots, and on the side, or in front, of the school building.[22]

How many civilian guns are there in the U.S.?

- As of 2017, there were an estimated *393 million guns* in civilian hands.[23]
- As of 2023, it is estimated to be at *466 million* due to increased sales during the pandemic.[24]

How many guns are not stored safely?

- *63%* of gun owners say they have at least one gun that is *never locked up*.[25]
- About *40%* of gun owners have at least one gun that is *loaded and easily accessible at all times*.[26]
- Roughly 4.6 million children live in a home with loaded and unlocked firearms.[27]
- An estimated 300,000 guns are stolen each year from private owners, more than 800 a day (2020).[28]

What states have the highest gun related mortality rates?[29]

- As of 2020, states with the highest gun-related mortality rates are *Mississippi, Louisiana, Wyoming, Missouri, Alabama, and Alaska.*
- States with the highest gun-related mortality rates are among the ones with the highest gun ownership rates.

What states have the fewest gun related deaths?[30]

- As of 2020, states with the lowest gun-related mortality rates are *Hawaii, Massachusetts, New Jersey, Rhode Island, and New York.*
- States with the lowest gun-related mortality rates had fewer gun ownership rates.

How does the U.S. compare to other countries in terms of deaths and gun ownership?

- The U.S. has far *higher rates of firearm death than any of the more than two dozen other high income countries* including: Australia, Canada, Germany, Italy, Japan, Norway, Spain, and the UK.[31]
- A correlated factor to firearm deaths is firearm possession, with it reported in 2017 that U.S. civilians had the *highest rate in the world of firearm possession.*[32]

What is known about the economic impact of gun violence?

- A 2019 report from the U.S. Congress Joint Economic Committee estimated that gun violence as *$229 billion a year* when considering lost income, employer costs, heath care, and police and criminal justice expenses.[33]
- Similarly, Everytown for Gun Safety estimates that amount to be $280 billion annually.[34]

How has the rate of U.S. gun deaths changed over time?

In 2022, the Johns Hopkins Bloomberg School of Public Health summarized "Gun Deaths Over the Last 40 Years" for suicide and homicide rates:[35]

- Overall, the firearm *suicide rate has not fluctuated significantly over the last 40 years.* Even in 2020, the firearm suicide rate remained at the same rate as in 1981.
- *Firearm homicide rates have fluctuated more than the suicide rate, although it is still lower than it was in the early 1990s.* Notably, in 2020 however, the gun homicide rate experienced the largest one-year increase in modern history.

Relative to Mass Shootings, the Gun Violence Archive reports that:

- Mass shooting rates have risen *from 272 in 2014 to 415 in 2019,* prior to the pandemic. Post pandemic there have been more than 600 annual mass shootings in 2020, 2021 and 2022.[36]

How do gun deaths compare to other leading causes of death?

- Based on 5-year averages in the U.S. there were:
  - 43,000 Gun deaths[37]
  - 37,000 Motor Vehicle deaths[38]
  - 43,000 Breast Cancer deaths[39]
  - 49,000 Pancreatic cancer deaths[40]
- Gun deaths are *the leading cause of death for children and teens* since 2020.[41] (Note that infants are not including in the category of children.)

WHAT IS KNOWN ABOUT GUN OWNERS?

What percent of Americans have at least gun in their household?

- 44% of Americans have at least one gun in their household, according to a Gallup poll in 2020.[42]
- About two-thirds of gun owners have more than one firearm, with the average gun owner having eight firearms.[43]
- Almost half of gun owners say that all or most of their friends own guns. Among those who don't own a gun, only about 10% say all or most of their friends own a gun.[44]

What is known about the reasons for owning a gun?

According to the Pew Research Center:[45]

- Most (67%) gun owners say the major reason they own a gun is for *protection*.
- More than a third (38%) indicate the major reason is for *hunting*, and almost a third (30%) for *sport shooting*.

What types of guns are owned?

- Among gunowners in 2020, 72% owned a handgun/pistol, 62% owned a rifle (including AR-15s), and 54% owned a shotgun.[46]

WHAT IS KNOWN ABOUT GUN SHOOTERS?

What is known about the profile of those *Committing Suicide*?

Everytown Research & Policy reports that firearm suicides have sharply divergent demographic rates:[47]

- *Males* represent 87% of firearm suicides.

- Firearm suicide rates increase with age, and especially high for *males 55 and older.*
- *Veterans* represent almost 18% of firearm suicides, even though they make up about 7% of the U.S. adult population.[48]
- *White Americans* represent 83% of all firearm suicide victims, with American Indians/Alaska Natives also disproportionately high with the second highest rate among the country's five major racial and ethnic groups.[49]
- Americans *living in rural areas* have far higher rates of firearm suicide than those living in urban areas, with rates 2.1 times higher in rural versus urban counties. Johns Hopkins Bloomberg School of Public Health notes that this significant difference may be correlated with more limited access to mental health services, high rates of alcohol use, and the highest rates of gun ownership.[50]

Additional informative facts from a variety of sources include:

- Most people who attempt suicide do not die unless they use a gun.[51]
- Increased access to mental health services may help prevent suicide deaths.[52]
- The vast majority of those surviving a suicide attempt do not go on to die by suicide.[53]

What is known about the profile of *Mass Shooters*?

A research report by Statista on a sampling of 142 mass shootings between 1982 and 2023 indicated the following by race, [54] with comparable proportions in the general population from 2022 U.S. Census Data. The fact that 10% were not known makes it difficult to draw conclusions related to racial profiles.[55]

- 52% of shooters were *White* vs. 59% of population

- 18% were *Black* vs. 14% of population
- 8% were *Latino* vs. 19% of population (Latino/Hispanic)
- 7% were *Asian* vs. 6% of population
- 2% were *Native American* vs. 1% of population
- 4% were Other
- 10% were Unknown/Unclear

For gender, the Statista report indicated that among mass shooters:[56]

- 96% were male (versus 49% of population)
- 3% were female
- 1% were male & female

For age, The Rockefeller Institute of Government reports:[57]

- The average age of mass shooters is 33.2 years old.

A 2022 National Institute of Justice study that conducted quantitative and qualitative research on mass shooters between 1966 and 1999 notes the following highlights:[58]

- Most had a prior criminal record (64.5%).
- Suicidality was found to be a strong predictor of mass shooters, with 30% suicidal prior to the shooting and 39% suicidal during the shooting.
- Nearly half of shooters (48%) "leaked" their plans in advance to others including family members, friends, and colleagues.
- 70% of mass shooters knew at least some of the victims.

What is known about the profile of *School Mass Shooters*?

Brookings Institution, a nonprofit public policy organization in Washington, DC, that conducts in-depth research regarding societal problems, reported in 2022 that:

- A majority of school shooters are reported as being male (95%) and white (61%).[59]
- K-12 shooters often report a history of rejection, have psychological problems (e.g., depression, suicidal ideation), and/or display a fascination with guns.[60]
- Many shooters communicate about their plans before the shooting (e.g., warn certain classmates not to attend school on a particular day).[61] In fact, the Department of Homeland Security reports that "93% of school shooters planned the attack in advance."[62] And "in 4 out of 5 school shootings, at least one other person had knowledge of the attacker's plan but failed to report it."[63]

In terms of age:

- Between 1970 and 2020, the highest number of school shootings were perpetrated by *17, 16 and 15-year olds.*[64]

WHAT IS KNOWN ABOUT OWNERSHIP OF GUNS THAT WERE USED?

Whose guns are used for Suicide?

- Among children and youth under 18, over 80% of firearm suicides involved *a gun belonging to a family member.*[65]
- APHA notes that "States with higher rates of gun ownership have higher suicide rates than states with low gun ownership ... indicating that *firearm access drives overall suicide rates.*"[66]

Whose guns are used for School Shootings?

- Almost *half of school shooters stole the gun from a family member.*[67]

WHAT IS KNOWN ABOUT HOMICIDE VICTIMS?

What is known about the profile of Homicide victims?

Homicide rates have increased 26% from 2010 to 2019, with one-third of all gun deaths categorized as homicides.[68] CDC's data include the following highlights for 2019, indicating rates disproportionately highest among:

- *Males,* at 84% of firearm homicide deaths. [69]
- *Black/African Americans,* at 53% of firearm homicide deaths.[70]
- *Youth,* with the highest risk age for dying by firearm homicide were *15-24 year olds.*[71]

When are women the most likely victims?

- On average, *every day, almost two women are killed by an intimate partner with a firearm.*[72]
- Between 1990 and 2021, about 14% of firearm deaths were women.[73]

Summary

In the end, these facts led to the prioritization in this book of four areas of focus for Social Marketing approaches to reducing gun deaths and gun injuries. They can be thought of as "The 4Ss":

- **Safe Gun Storage:** This area of primary focus is inspired by the data mentioned that almost half of school shooters stole the gun from a family member;[74] and among children and youth under 18, over 80% of firearm suicides involved a gun belonging to a family member.[75] In addition, 63% of gun owners say they have at least one gun that is never locked up,[76] and about 40% have at least one gun that is loaded and easily accessible.[77]

- **Suicide Prevention**: The majority, more than 60%, of firearm deaths with intent each year are a result of suicides.[78] Most who attempt suicide do not die unless they use a gun.[79] And the vast majority of those surviving a suicide attempt do not go on to die by suicide.[80] An intervention is key.
- **Say Something If See Something:** This act can have a huge impact given that nearly half of mass shooters (48%) "leaked" their plans in advance to others including family members, friends, and colleagues.[81] And "in 4 out of 5 school shootings, at least one other person had knowledge of the attacker's plan but failed to report it."[82]
- **Social Equity Lens:** Given the disproportionate gender, race, age, and poverty levels of offenders, as well as victims, program planners and campaign managers need to use a social equity lens when developing interventions that will have the most impact, such as the data from Johns Hopkins that states that young black males (15-34) accounted for 38% of all gun homicide fatalities in 2020 and yet they represent only 2% of the total U.S. population.[83]

References

1 The Guardian, "Texas gunman allegedly texted German teenager plans for attack" (May 2022), accessed at https://www.theguardian.com/us-news/2022/may/26/texas-shooter-texted-german-teenager-plans

2 Sandy Hook Promise, " Say Something Creates Cultural Change That Leads To Safer Schools" (2022), accessed September 28, 2022, https://www.sandyhookpromise.org/our-programs/say-something/

3 Sandy Hook Promise, "17 Facts About Gun Violence And School shootings" (2023), accessed at https://www.sandyhookpromise.org/our-programs/say-something/

4 BROOKINGS, "School shootings: What we know about them, and what we can do to prevent them" (January 2022), R. Kowalski, accessed at https://www.brookings.edu/blog/brown-center-chalkboard/2022/01/26/school-shootings-what-we-know-about-them-and-what-we-can-do-to-prevent-them/

5 EFSBV, "A Public Health Crisis Decades in the Making: A Review of 2019 CDC Gun Mortality Data" (February 2021), p.6, accessed at http://efsgv.org/2019CDCdata

6 Everytown for Gun Safety, "Debunking gun Myths at the Dinner Table" (October 2022), accessed at https://www.everytown.org/debunking-gun-myths-at-the-dinner-table/

7 Pew Research Center, "What the data says about gun deaths in the U.S." (February 2022), J. Gramlich, accessed at https://www.pewresearch.org/short-reads/2023/04/26/what-the-data-says-about-gun-deaths-in-the-u-s/

8 Johns Hopkins Bloomberg School of Public Health, "A Year in Review. 2020 Gun Deaths in the U.S." (April 2022), accessed at https://publichealth.jhu.edu/sites/default/files/2022-05/2020-gun-deaths-in-the-us-4-28-2022-b.pdf

9 CNN health, "Children and teens are more likely to die by gun than anything else" (March 2023), accessed at https://www.cnn.com/2023/03/29/health/us-children-gun-deaths-dg/index.html

10 EFSBV, "A Public Health Crisis Decades in the Making: A Review of 2019 CDC Gun Mortality Data" (February 2021), p.7, accessed at http://efsgv.org/2019CDCdata

[11] Police Executive Research Forum, "Reducing Gun Violence: What Works, and What Can Be Done Now" (March 2019), p.4, accessed at https://www.police forum.org/assets/reducinggunviolence.pdf

[12] EFSBV, "Firearm Homicide" (February 2021), accessed at https://efsgv.org/learn/type-of-gun-violence/firearm-homicide/

[13] EFSBV, "A Public Health Crisis Decades in the Making: A Review of 2019 CDC Gun Mortality Data" (February 2021), p.6, accessed at http://efsgv.org/2019CDCdata

[14] Ibid. p.8

[15] CNN, "Mass Shootings in the US Fast Facts" (May 2023), accessed at https://www.cnn.com/2023/01/24/us/mass-shootings-fast-facts/index.html

[16] Ibid.

[17] EFSBV, "A Public Health Crisis Decades in the Making: A Review of 2019 CDC Gun Mortality Data" (February 2021), p.5, accessed at http://efsgv.org/2019CDCdata

[18] USA FACTS, "The latest government data on school shootings" (April 2023), accessed at https://usafacts.org/articles/the-latest-government-data-on-school-shootings/

[19] Ibid.

[20] Reuters, "Factbox: U.S. states with the most and fewest school shootings" (May 2019), accessed at https://www.reuters.com/article/us-colorado-shooting-states-factbox-idUSKCN1SE2EX

[21] Ibid.

[22] USA FACTS, "The latest government data on school shootings" (April 2023), accessed at https://usafacts.org/articles/the-latest-government-data-on-school-shootings/

[23] American Gun Facts, "How Man Guns are in the US?" (March 2023), accessed at https://americangunfacts.com/gun-ownership-statistics/

[24] Ibid.

[25] Reader's Digest, "Guns in America", (Nov. 2022), D. Saldana, accessed at https://www.rd.com/article/gun-violence-statistics/

[26] Ibid.

[27] npr, "6 major takeaways from the ATF's first report in 20 years on U.S. gun crime" (February 2023), J. Diaz, accessed at https://www.npr.org/2023/02/10/1153977949/major-takeaways-from-the-atf-gun-violence-report

[28] The Trace, "How Many Guns Fall Out of Circulation Each Year In the U.S."" (October 2021), accessed at https://www.thetrace.org/2021/10/firearm-average-lifespan-how-many-lost-stolen-broken-guns

[29] CNN, "States with the most gun violence share one trait" (May 2022), accessed at https://www.cnn.com/2022/05/26/politics/gun-violence-data-what-matters/index.html

[30] Ibid.

[31] HARVARD Magazine, "Forum: Doing Less Harm" (February 2020), D. Hemenway, accessed at https://www.harvardmagazine.com/2020/01/gun-violence-control

[32] U.S. News, "U.S. Remains an Outlier in Firearm Possession, Gun-Related Deaths" (January 2023), C. Gilligan, accessed at https://www.usnews.com/news/best-countries/articles/2023-01-30/how-the-u-s-compares-to-the-world-on-guns

[33] Reader's Digest, "Guns in America", (Nov. 2022), D. Saldana, accessed at https://www.rd.com/article/gun-violence-statistics/

[34] Ibid.

[35] Johns Hopkins Bloomberg School of Public Health, "A Year in Review. 2020 Gun Deaths in the U.S." (April 2022) p.7-9, accessed at https://publichealth.jhu.edu/sites/default/files/2022-05/2020-gun-deaths-in-the-us-4-28-2022-b.pdf

[36] CNN, "Mass Shootings in the U.S. Fast Facts" (January 2023), accessed at https://www.cnn.com/2023/01/24/us/mass-shootings-fast-facts/index.html

[37] Reader's Digest, "Guns in America", (Nov. 2022), D. Saldana, accessed at https://www.rd.com/article/gun-violence-statistics/

[38] WIKIPEDIA, "Motor vehicle fatality fare in U.S. by year" (April 2023), accessed at https://en.wikipedia.org/wiki/Motor_vehicle_fatality_rate_in_U.S._by_year

[39] Reader's Digest, "Guns in America", (Nov. 2022), D. Saldana, accessed at https://www.rd.com/article/gun-violence-statistics/

[40] Ibid.

[41] CNN health, "Children and teens are more likely to die by gun than anything else" (March 2023), accessed at https://www.cnn.com/2023/03/29/health/us-children-gun-deaths-dg/index.html

[42] Reader's Digest, "Guns in America", (Nov. 2022), D. Saldana, accessed at https://www.rd.com/article/gun-violence-statistics/

[43] Ibid.

[44] Pew Research Center, "America's Complex Relationship With Guns" (June 2017), K. Parker et al., accessed at https://www.pewresearch.org/social-trends/2017/06/22/americas-complex-relationship-with-guns/

[45] Pew Research Center, "Key takeaways on Americans' views of guns and gun ownership" (June 2017), R. Igielnik and A. Brown, accessed at

https://www.pewresearch.org/short-reads/2017/06/22/key-takeaways-on-americans-views-of-guns-and-gun-ownership/

[46] Reader's Digest, "Guns in America", (Nov. 2022), D. Saldana, accessed at https://www.rd.com/article/gun-violence-statistics/

[47] EVERYTOWN, "Firearm Suicides in the United States" (February 2023), accessed at https://everytownresearch.org/report/firearm-suicide-in-the-united-states/

[48] BRADY, "Firearm Suicide Risk Among Veterans and Military Service Members" (2019), accessed at https://www.bradyunited.org/fact-sheets/veterans-and-suicide

[49] EVERYTOWN, "Firearm Suicides in the United States" (February 2023), accessed at https://everytownresearch.org/report/firearm-suicide-in-the-united-states/

[50] Ibid.

[51] Johns Hopkins Bloomberg School of Public Health, "A Year in Review. 2020 Gun Deaths in the U.S." (April 2022) p.27, accessed at https://publichealth.jhu.edu/sites/default/files/2022-05/2020-gun-deaths-in-the-us-4-28-2022-b.pdf

[52] EVERYTOWN, "Firearm Suicides in the United States" (February 2023), accessed at https://everytownresearch.org/report/firearm-suicide-in-the-united-states/

[53] Ibid.

[54] statista, "Number of mass shootings in the U.S. between 1932 and April 2023, by shooter's race or ethnicity." (2023), accessed at https://www.statista.com/statistics/476456/mass-shootings-in-the-us-by-shooter-s-race/

[55] United States Census, "QuickFacts" (July 2022), accessed at https://www.census.gov/quickfacts/US

[56] statista, "Number of mass shootings in the U.S. by gender" (2023), accessed at https://www.statista.com/statistics/476445/mass-shootings-in-the-us-by-shooter-s-gender/

[57] Rockefeller Institute of Government, "Mass Shooting Factsheet" (2022), accessed at https://rockinst.org/gun-violence/mass-shooting-factsheet/

[58] NIJ, "Public Mass Shootings: Database Amasses Detail of a Half Century of U.S. Mass Shootings with Firearms, Generating Psychosocial Histories" (February, 2022), accessed at https://nij.ojp.gov/topics/articles/public-mass-shootings-database-amasses-details-half-century-us-mass-shootings

[59] BROOKINGS, "School shootings: What we know about them, and what we can do to prevent them" (January 2022), R. Kowalski, accessed at https://www.brookings.edu/blog/brown-center-chalkboard/2022/01/26/

school-shootings-what-we-know-about-them-and-what-we-can-do-to-prevent-them/

[60] Ibid.

[61] Ibid.

[62] Sandy Hook Promise, " Say Something Creates Cultural Change That Leads To Safer Schools" (2022), accessed September 28, 2022, https://www.sandy hookpromise.org/our-programs/say-something/

[63] Ibid.

[64] Statista, "Number of K-12 school shootings in the United States from 1970 to June 16, 2020, by age of shooter" (2023), https://www.statista.com/ statistics/971544/number-k-12-school-shootings-us-age-shooter/

[65] EVERYTOWN, "Firearm Suicides in the United States" (February 2023), accessed at https://everytownresearch.org/report/firearm-suicide-in-the-united-states/

[66] APHA, "Reducing Suicides by Firearms" (November 2018), accessed at https://www.apha.org/policies-and-advocacy/public-health-policy-statements/policy-database/2019/01/28/reducing-suicides-by-firearms

[67] BROOKINGS, "School shootings: What we know about them, and what we can do to prevent them" (January 2022), R. Kowalski, accessed at https://www.brookings.edu/blog/brown-center-chalkboard/2022/01/26/ school-shootings-what-we-know-about-them-and-what-we-can-do-to-prevent-them/

[68] EFSBV, "Firearm Homicide" (February 2021), accessed at https://efsgv .org/learn/type-of-gun-violence/firearm-homicide/

[69] Ibid.

[70] Ibid.

[71] Ibid.

[72] CAP, "Guns and Violence Against Women" (January 2022), accessed at https://www.americanprogress.org/article/guns-and-violence-against-women/

[73] Sheknows, "Gun Deaths in the U.S. Have Skyrocketed, Especially Among Women," (December 2022), accessed at https://www.sheknows.com/ health-and-wellness/articles/2675617/gun-deaths-skyrocketing-women-study/

[74] BROOKINGS, "School shootings: What we know about them, and what we can do to prevent them" (January 2022), R. Kowalski, accessed at https://www.brookings.edu/blog/brown-center-chalkboard/2022/01/26/ school-shootings-what-we-know-about-them-and-what-we-can-do-to-prevent-them/

[75] EVERYTOWN, "Firearm Suicides in the United States" (February 2023), accessed at https://everytownresearch.org/report/firearm-suicide-in-the-united-states/

[76] Reader's Digest, "Guns in America", (Nov. 2022), D. Saldana, accessed at https://www.rd.com/article/gun-violence-statistics/

[77] Ibid.

[78] EFSBV, "A Public Health Crisis Decades in the Making: A Review of 2019 CDC Gun Mortality Data" (February 2021), p.5, accessed at http://efsgv.org/2019CDCdata

[79] EVERYTOWN, "Firearm Suicides in the United States" (February 2023), accessed at https://everytownresearch.org/report/firearm-suicide-in-the-united-states/

[80] Ibid.

[81] NIJ, "Public Mass Shootings: Database Amasses Detail of a Half Century of U.S. Mass Shootings with Firearms, Generating Psychosocial Histories" (February, 2022), accessed at https://nij.ojp.gov/topics/articles/public-mass-shootings-database-amasses-details-half-century-us-mass-shootings

[82] Sandy Hook Promise, "17 Facts About Gun Violence And School shootings" (2023), accessed at 17 Facts About Gun Violence And School Shootings — Sandy Hook Promise

[83] Johns Hopkins Bloomberg School of Public Health, "A Year in Review. 2020 Gun Deaths in the U.S." (April 2022) p.7-9, accessed at https://public health.jhu.edu/sites/default/files/2022-05/2020-gun-deaths-in-the-us-4-28-2022-b.pdf

Chapter 2

A Social Marketing Approach
Behavior Change for Good

Social Marketing Defined

The discipline of Social Marketing was first distinguished more than 50 years ago by Professors Philip Kotler at Northwestern University, and Gerald Zaltman at Harvard University, in an article in the *Journal of Marketing* in 1971, "Social Marketing: An Approach to Planned Social Change." The article addressed the question: "Can marketing concepts and techniques be effectively applied to the promotion of social objectives such as brotherhood, safe driving, and family planning? ... The authors show how social causes can be advanced more successfully through applying principles of marketing analysis, planning, and control to problems of social change."[1]

Defined more formally by the International Social Marketing Association as of 2023:

> "Social marketing seeks to develop and integrate marketing concepts with other approaches to influence behaviours that benefit individuals and communities for the greater social good." [2]

Over the past 50 years this behavior change approach has been used to improve public *health* (e.g., reducing the spread of COVID-19), prevent *injuries* (e.g., reducing youth suicides), protect the *environment* (e.g., increasing recycling), and engage *communities* (e.g., increasing blood donations). As of 2022, there are 8 Global Professional Marketing Membership Associations, an estimated 2,500 Social Marketing Association Members around the world, more than 40 books with Social Marketing titles, 2 Academic Journals, and academic course offerings around the globe.[3]

In terms of related terminology:

> Some might think of social marketing as a *Public Health Approach,* such as one to reduce gun violence. As the Johns Hopkins Center for Gun Violence Solutions elaborates: "Gun violence is a public health epidemic ... The public health approach addresses the many forms of gun violence by focusing both on firearm access and underlying risk factors that contribute to gun violence ... By using a public health approach, we can prevent gun violence in all its forms and strive towards health equity, where everyone can live free from gun violence."[4] Social marketing can be thought of as a relevant discipline to be employed, given that behavior change is its objective.

> It wouldn't be surprising if, when you first heard the term Social Marketing, you assumed it to be the same as *Social Media.* You're not alone. The distinction between the two is that social media is a tactic that social marketers, and others, use to influence priority audiences. But it is only "an attachment" to one of the 4 major intervention tools, *Promotion,* that marketers use to influence a desired action. Behavior change takes more than communication. It almost always takes all 4Ps, with the other standard influential marketing tools being the *Product, Price,* and *Place* that are then *Promoted.*

How Social Marketing is Distinct from other Behavior Change Approaches to Reducing Gun Violence

When a behavior change idea is introduced into the marketplace (e.g., wear a mask when out in public to protect yourself and others from the spread of COVID-19), there are likely to be three distinct population segments to consider when developing strategies, ones based on "readiness to change."[5] Using COVID-19 as an example, and descriptions of segments presented in Figure 2.1:

- *The Show Me Group* thinks this behavior is a good idea and is ready to go find and wear a mask. All they need to act is **Education**, like information on how to get one quickly and when to wear it. As implied by the graphic, unfortunately these early adopters are typically a small group.
- *The Help Me Group*, often the largest group for social marketing-related behaviors, is one that is open to doing a behavior to advance social good, but has concerns and considerations such as whether the mask actually works to protect from COVID, how much it costs, whether they are available locally, and how they will be perceived by others when wearing a mask. A **Social Marketing** intervention is needed for this group, one that provides viable products, price incentives, convenient places to get one, and persuasive promotions to help address each of their concerns.
- *The Make Me Group* is not at all interested in the proposed behavior, seeing the Pandemic as a hoax, an expression of governmental control, and the mask as looking ridiculous. Until it becomes required by **Law**, behavior adoption is very unlikely for this group. Typically, however, it is thankfully a small group relative to social marketing-related behaviors.

Figure 2.1 *Approaches to Behavior Change: Education, Social Marketing and Law*

Source: C+C Communications Agency

Figure 2.1 illustrates a framework that identifies and distinguishes between three approaches to influencing behavior change for social good. The model is inspired by the Diffusion of Innovations Theory, one developed by Everett Rogers that identified five different population segments based on points in time when an innovation is accepted: Innovators, Early Adopters, Early Majority, Late Majority and Laggards. [6] This Figure was adapted from a model reinterpreted by Jay Kassirer, Mike Rothschild, Dave Ward, and designed by C+C in Seattle. [7]

Relative to reducing gun deaths and injuries, the following summaries provide examples and distinctions for Education, Social Marketing and Law strategies.

The Education Approach

Education strategies focus on providing information that increases awareness and concern about the nature of and prevalence of gun violence. Relative to gun deaths and injuries, examples include:

- Daily News segments that describe a recent gun violent act such as a mass shooting, noting location, time of day, profile of the victim, and anything that is known about the shooter.
- Annual Reports that summarize the number of victims of gun violence, types of guns that were used, profile of offenders, and locations where shootings occurred.

What is not highlighted in an Education strategy are recommended protective behaviors and resources for taking action.

The Social Marketing Approach

A social marketing strategy focuses on inspiring those who are aware and concerned about gun violence to take protective actions such as storing guns in homes safely. "Help" to do this is then provided, falling into one or more of the 4P categories:

- *Products*: Providing options and descriptions of safe gun storage solutions
- *Price*: Offering incentives such as gift cards given at a gun buy-back program in exchange for a gun
- *Place*: Providing gun cable locks at a local city police station
- *Promotion*: Including more information on news casts about shootings that would motivate protective behaviors such as evidence that the offender had stolen the gun from a family member, and had let a friend know in advance of their planned shooting

The Law Approach

Examples of laws to help reduce gun violence include:

- Red Flag Laws in some states permitting a state court to order temporary removal of firearms from a person who may present a danger to others or themselves[8]
- The Vote Without Fear Act, passed in Colorado in 2022, prohibiting openly carrying a firearm at polling locations or central count facilities[9]

Examples of legislative acts/bills that have been proposed by some lawmakers, but not passed at the time this book was published, are ones such as the following, seen as ways to reduce gun deaths and injuries:[10]

- Raise the purchasing age for semiautomatic rifles from 18-21.
- Outlaw the import, sale, manufacture, transfer or possession of high-capacity magazines, bump stocks.
- Regulate storage of firearms on residential premises to be safely stored if a minor is able to gain access without permission.

A Ten Step Social Marketing Planning Framework

Table 2.1 provides an outline of a framework for developing a strategic social marketing plan, one originally developed by Nancy Lee and Philip Kotler, and adapted from a version published in *Social Marketing: Behavior Change for Good* 7th Edition (SAGE 2024).[11]

Table 2.1   A TEN STEP PLAN SOCIAL MARKETING PLANNING FRAMEWORK

1.0   **Social Issue, DEI Considerations, Organization(s), Background, Purpose, and Focus**
 1.1   Social issue plan is intended to impact
 1.2   Diversity, equity, and inclusion (DEI) considerations relevant to the social issue
 1.3   Organization(s) involved in developing and implementing plan
 1.4   Background information leading to the development of this plan
 1.5   Purpose of this effort, relative to the social issue
 1.6   Focus, the approach this plan will take to contribute to the purpose

2.0   **Situation Analysis (SWOT)**
 2.1   Organizational strengths (e.g., management priority)
 2.2   Organizational weaknesses (e.g., funding limitations)
 2.3   External opportunities (e.g., levels of societal concern)
 2.4   External threats (e.g., advocates for competing issues)
 2.5   Key learnings from review of similar prior efforts

3.0   **Priority Audience**
 3.1   Description of priority audience for this plan including: relevant demographics, geographics, readiness to change, current related behaviors, values and lifestyle, and social networks
 3.2   Additional important audiences that you will need to influence

4.0   **Objectives and Goals**
 4.1   Behavior Objective, one intended for the priority audience to be influenced to adopt
 4.2   Knowledge Objective, what your audience needs to know in order to be more likely to act
 4.3   Belief Objective, what your audience needs to believe in order to be more likely to act
 4.4   SMART Goals (Specific, Measurable, Achievable, Relevant, Time-bound) quantifying levels of desired behavior change outcomes as well as changes in knowledge, beliefs, and behavior intent

5.0   **Priority Audience Barriers, Benefits, Motivators, Competition, and Influential Others**
 5.1   Perceived barriers and costs associated with adopting the desired behavior
 5.2   Desired benefits in exchange for performing the desired behavior
 5.3   Potential strategies the priority audience identifies that might motivate them to perform the behavior
 5.4   Competing behaviors/forces/choices
 5.5   Those who the priority audience is most likely to be influenced by to perform the behavior

Table 2.1   A TEN STEP PLAN SOCIAL MARKETING PLANNING FRAMEWORK

6.0   Positioning Statement

How you want the priority audience to see the desired behavior, highlighting desired benefits and motivators

7.0   Marketing Intervention Mix (4Ps)

7.1   **Product:** *Benefits from performing behaviors and features of goods and services offered to assist adoption*
Core Product: Audience-desired benefits for performing the behavior
Actual Product: Features of any tangible goods or services offered/promoted
Augmented Product: Additional goods and services to help increase appeal

7.2   **Price:** *Costs that will be associated with adopting the behavior and tactics to reduce costs or increase benefiits*
- Monetary incentives (e.g., discounts, rebates)
- Nonmonetary incentives (e.g., pledges, recognition, appreciation)
- Monetary disincentives (e.g., fines)
- Nonmonetary disincentives (e.g., negative public visibility)

7.3   **Place:** Where and when audiences will perform the behavior or access any goods and services

7.4   **Promotion:** Persuasive communications highlighting the offer: product, price, and place strategies
- Messages
- Messengers
- Creative strategies
- Communication channels including any prompts for sustainability

8.0   Evaluation Plan

8.1   Purpose of evaluation
8.2   Audience for whom evaluation is being conducted
8.3   What will be measured: inputs, outputs, outcomes (from Step 4), and (potentially impact and return on investment
8.4   How measures will be taken
8.5   When measures will be taken
8.6   How much evaluation will cost

9.0   Budget

Costs of implementing marketing plan, including a pilot and evaluation plan
Include any incremental revenues, cost savings, and partner contributions

10.0   Implementation Plan

Who will do what, when, for how much – including any partners and their roles
Pilot projects are strongly encouraged prior to full implementation, informing any changes for a roll out.

Summary

Stated simply, the Social Marketing approach for reducing gun deaths and injuries uses more than Education (information and facts), as it also includes recommended behaviors to perform and strategies to make it more likely. And it differs from Laws and Policies to influence change, as behaviors that are promoted using a social marketing approach are voluntary.

References

[1] Internet Archive Scholar, "Social Marketing: An Approach to Planned Social Change", P. Kotler and G. Zaltman, accessed at https://scholar.archive.org/work/yhctwnuznncwxednusxmbi6lli

[2] N. Lee, P. Kotler, and J. Colehour, *Social Marketing: Behavior Change for Good*, 7th Ed. (Thousand Oaks, CA: SAGE PUBLICATIONS, 2024), p.6.

[3] Ibid., p.437.

[4] EFSGV, "Public Health Approach to Gun Violence Prevention" (2017), p.1, accessed at https://efsgv.org/learn/learn-more-about-gun-violence/public-health-approach-to-gun-violence-prevention/

[5] N. Lee, P. Kotler, and J. Colehour, *Social Marketing: Behavior Change for Good*, 7th Ed. (Thousand Oaks, CA: SAGE PUBLICATIONS, 2024), pp.133-134.

[6] Ibid., pp. 77-78.

[7] Ibid., p.134.

[8] WIKIPEDIA, "Red flag law" (May 2023), accessed at https://en.wikipedia.org/wiki/Red_flag_law

[9] CNN, "These are the gun control laws passed in 2022" (December 2022), accessed at https://www.cnn.com/2022/07/30/us/gun-control-laws-2022/index.html

[10] CNBC, "House Democrats look to pass gun control legislation by early June" (May 31, 2022), accessed at https://www.cnbc.com/2022/05/31/house-democrats-aim-to-pass-gun-control-legislation-by-early-june.html

[11] N. Lee, P. Kotler, and J. Colehour, *Social Marketing: Behavior Change for Good*, 7th Ed. (Thousand Oaks, CA: SAGE PUBLICATIONS, 2024), pp.32-33.

Chapter 3

Gun Owners
Storing Guns Safely to Reduce
Youth/Children Gun Suicides

Background, Purpose & Focus

Several statistics for the U.S. in 2019 confirm the importance of efforts to prevent suicide gun deaths:

- 61% of all gun deaths in the U.S. are suicides. [1]
- Approximately 90% of suicide attempts involving a gun end in death. [2]
- Nearly 23,000 Americans died by firearm suicide. [3]
- An average of 63 people a day died by firearm suicide. [4]

The following statistics in 2016 confirm the importance of campaigns with a *purpose* to reduce *youth/children suicide deaths from firearms*: [5]

- Among youth/children 1-19, there were 3143 firearm deaths
- 35% of these (1102) were the result of suicide.
- An average of 3 youth/children died every day by firearm suicide.

And the facts that over 80% of firearm suicides by youth/children in the U.S. involve a gun belonging to a family member, relative or friend; [6] 44% of Americans have at least one gun in their household, according to a Gallup poll in 2020; [7] and 45% of gun owners with youth/children under 18 in the home reported not storing all guns safely inspired the *focus* of this chapter on *safe home gun storage*. [8]

A Social Marketing Approach

An article published by Johns Hopkins Bloomberg School of Public Health states that: "Safe gun storage refers to practices that limit accessibility to guns by unauthorized users and has the potential to reduce gun-related injuries and deaths. Safe storage best practices include locking guns in a secure place such as a gun safe or cabinet, or using safety devices such as trigger or cable locks."[9] And the Office of Violence Prevention in Austin, Texas, states that: "Data suggests that a modest increase in the number of Americans that safely store firearms could prevent almost *a third of youth/children gun deaths* due to suicide and unintentional firearm injury." [10]

Priority Audience & Desired Behavior

Based on this data, it is not surprising that many, if not most, efforts to increase safe gun storage prioritize *gunowners with youth/children in their home* to *safely secure and/or store their guns*. The specific desired behaviors include those that will reduce the risk of unauthorized access or use, and include options of putting guns in a gun safe or locked cabinet, installing safety devices such as a trigger or cable lock, and locking into a gun rack.

Audience Insights

A national survey conducted for Johns Hopkins Bloomberg School of Public Health in 2018 revealed many of the following inspiring audience insights related to gun storage to protect family members:[11]

- *Barriers* noted in survey results included the finding that 43% of gun owners were concerned that if they locked up their guns, they wouldn't have quick and easy access to firearms in cases of home intrusions.

- *Benefits* that might outweigh their concerns were focused on the safety of their family.
- *Motivators* to be considered included instructions and perhaps trainings related to options for safely securing their firearms; what options were best to ensure home safety in the event of an intruder; and how to have discussions with family members that would confirm safe storage is a good idea.
- *Influencers* that respondents saw as most credible were law enforcement officials, with 77% in agreement with this option.

An additional insight, relative to a focus on suicide prevention, was an article published by Brady United that offered insight as to why some gun owners might not be motivated to secure their firearms to specifically help prevent youth suicide. "67% of Americans mistakenly believe that most people who survive a suicide attempt will make additional attempts in the future." [12] It would be motivating however for them to learn that "In fact, 70% never attempt suicide again."[13] Implications are that preventing even a first attempt by securing guns can help prevent future attempts that might result in a death.

Key Strategies & Results

Three efforts to increase safe firearm storage are featured in this section, ones designed to overcome barriers (e.g., not having a safe storage device); highlight benefits (e.g., saving the lives of youth/children); increasing the practice as a perceived community norm (e.g., a variety of organizations using similar messaging strategies for their efforts); and making access to safe storage devices "free and easy."

Michigan: Free Gun Trigger-Locks[14]

An article in the *Journal of Applied Communication Research* highlighted a campaign in Michigan to inspire gun owners to secure their firearms by increasing knowledge of the danger to youth/children from an unlocked and loaded gun, and to make it free and easy to receive a gun trigger-lock. A radio PSA focused on the specific dangers to youth/children from an unlocked and loaded gun in the home, and at the end of the message, a toll-free number was provided to call to receive a free gun trigger-lock.

"Seven-hundred and ninety-nine individuals called the *toll-free number* to receive a free gun trigger-lock, approximately 17 percent of gun-owning households exposed to the message. The majority of callers were males who owned guns primarily for hunting purposes and who planned to use the lock themselves. Follow-up survey results indicated that individuals were using the gun trigger-locks, and that they believed using gun trigger-locks was an easy and effective way to prevent gun injuries."[15] In addition, surveys were conducted that indicated approximately 20 percent of the general population had heard the radio PSA. Findings indicated that among those recalling the campaign, there was an increase in knowledge of the locking-related gun-safety practices.

Texas: Safe Gun Storage Saves Lives Campaigns

A March 2022 news story in Austin, Texas, reported that "Nationally, more than half of gun owners store at least one gun unsafely. And according to the CDC, in 2019, 3,683 deaths in Texas were due to firearms – above the national rate and rising each year since 2011."[16] The story also noted that a new *Safe Gun Storage Saves Lives* campaign will be a first-of-its-kind collaboration by the nonprofit Lock Arms for Life with governmental agencies including Texas Department of Public Safety, Austin Police Department,

Austin Public Health Office of Violence Prevention, and the Travis County District Attorney's Office. The following efforts in Austin demonstrate the potential impact of aligning key organizations such as these in a community to ensure widespread outreach, a variety of strategic intervention tools, influential messengers, and consistent messaging.

- The Texas Department of Public Safety created a robust media campaign featuring the slogan, *Keep 'Em Safe Texas* and a website https://safegunstoragetexas.com that provides accessible protective resources including *printable safe gun storage checklists, testimonial videos* featuring real stories from real people, and tools on *how to talk to others* about safe gun storage. Materials are provided in both English and Spanish.[17]
- Austin Public Health teamed up with the nonprofit Lock Arms for Life to provide *free gun locks* to residents and are made available at special events, police departments and through the campaign's website.
- The Office of Violence Prevention partnered with Lock Arms for Life to connect families in Central Texas with the education and resources needed to safely store firearms.
- The Austin Police Department provides free gun locks at a variety of their police stations.

Leesa Ross, Director of Lock Arms for Life, reported that billboards in well-traveled areas received more than 5 million impressions, and that bus ads and inside cards generated an estimated 1.67 million impressions (See Figure 3.1) . In the last 5 years the organization as distributed about 2500 gun locks and 150 lock boxes.[18]

Figure 3.1 *Lock Arms for Life Media Campaign*

Source: Leesa Ross, Director of Lock Arms for Life

Ad Council & Brady United: Tips and Resources[19]

In 2018 Brady United, a gun violence prevention group, and the Ad Council launched a nationwide *End Family Fire* campaign to bring greater attention to gun suicide and the role that safe gun storage plays in its prevention. And in 2020, a new suite of PSAs, created pro bono by ad agency McKinney, included:

- TV and social media video spots
- Radio spots featuring voices of real people who lost loved ones to gun suicide
- Print, digital and out-of-home ads that "share eye-opening statistics, including the stark fact that 63 people a day die from gun suicide in the U.S."[20]

All PSAs encourage gun owners to store firearms locked, unloaded, and separate from ammunition, and to visit EndFamilyFire.org for tips and resources such as the National Suicide Prevention Lifeline.

"Since the campaign's launch, parents in households with guns who are aware of the campaign are more than twice as likely to have sought information about safe gun storage in the past year (36% among campaign-aware compared to 17% of those who are not campaign-aware)."[21]

Applicable Behavior Change Theories

The *Social Cognitive Theory*[22] states there are two major factors that will increase the likelihood of influencing a priority audience to take a preventive action such as safe gun storage. One is related to the person's belief that the *benefits of performing the behavior will outweigh the costs*, similar to the *Exchange Theory*. Campaigns noted in this chapter addressed this factor by highlighting that saving a family member's life is worth the efforts to acquire safety devices and safely store guns. A second factor is whether the person believes that he or she has the skills and ability to perform the behavior. Similarly, efforts highlighted in this chapter provided multiple intervention tools to increase competence including instructional videos, checklists, and demonstrations at special events.

The *Health Belief Model*[23] suggests that the probability of adopting a behavior will be influenced by several factors, including the following five illustrated with relevant safe gun storage implications:

- Perceived Susceptibility: "Will my child really ever actually try to get a hold of my gun?"
- Perceived Severity: "If my child got a hold of my gun, what might they do with it?"
- Perceived Benefits of Taking Action: "If the gun is stored safely, could it save my child's life?"
- Perceived Barriers to Taking Action: "What if an intruder with a gun gets in my home, won't it take too long for me to

access my gun? How hard is it to secure my gun and, if I want to, can I get storage equipment easily and cheap?"

- Cues to Action: "Are there any organizations and respected members of my community that are highlighting this issue, and recommending safe gun storage to help prevent youth suicides?"

Social Marketing Principles Contributing to Success[24]

The application of several key social marketing principles were apparent in this chapter's featured efforts:

- The *priority audience* of gunowners with children/youth in the home and an unlocked gun meets key factors to consider when selecting a priority audience including: significant size, problem incidence, readiness to act, ability to reach, and a good match for the organizations sponsoring this effort.
- A *single, clear desired behavior* to safely secure and/or store their guns is consistently promoted by a variety of organizations.
- *Highlighting the primary desired benefit* of protecting their family was central to establishing a belief that benefits will outweigh the costs.
- Barriers to safe gun storage were addressed by making *products* (e.g., gun trigger-locks) *accessible, easy to use,* and often *free*.
- Collaboration among nonprofit organizations and governmental agencies contributed to increased visibility and support for the desired behavior of safe gun storage, helping to establish a *perceived social norm* for safe gun storage.

References

[1] EFSBV, "A Public Health Crisis Decades in the Making: A Review of 2019 CDC Gun Mortality Data" (February 2021), p.7, accessed at http://efsgv.org/2019CDCdata.

[2] Police Executive Research Forum, "Reducing Gun Violence: What Works, and What Can Be Done Now" (March 2019), accessed at https://www.police forum.org/assets/reducinggunviolence.pdf.

[3] EFSBV, "A Public Health Crisis Decades in the Making: A Review of 2019 CDC Gun Mortality Data" (February 2021), p.7, accessed at http://efsgv .org/2019CDCdata.

[4] Ibid.

[5] New England Journal of Medicine, "Major Causes of Death in Children and Adolescents in the United States" (December 20, 2018) R. Cunningham, et al., accessed at https://www.nejm.org/doi/full/10.1056 /NEJMsr1804754

[6] Children's Hospital of Philadelphia, "Safe Storage of Guns in the Home" (January 2022), accessed at https://violence.chop.edu/gun-violence-facts-and-statistics .

[7] Reader's Digest, "Guns in America", (Nov. 2022), D. Saldana, accessed at https://www.rd.com/article/gun-violence-statistics/

[8] Johns Hopkins Bloomberg School of Public Health, "Safe Gun Storage" (n.d.), accessed at https://www.jhsph.edu/research/centers-and-institutes/johns-hopkins-center-for-gun-violence-prevention-and-policy/research/safe-gun-storage/

[9] Ibid.

[10] City of Austin Office of Violence Prevention, "Office of Violence Prevention Partners with Lock Arms for Life for Safe Gun Storage Campaign" (March, 2022), accessed at https://www.austintexas.gov/news/office-violence-prevention-partners-lock-arms-life-safe-gun-storage-campaign

[11] Johns Hopkins Bloomberg School of Public Health, "Survey: More Than Half of U.S. Gun Owners Do Not Safely Store Their Guns" (February 22, 2018), accessed at https://publichealth.jhu.edu/2018/survey-more-than-half-of-u-s-gun-owners-do-not-safely-store-their-guns

[12] The Brady Campaign and the Ad Council, "New National Campaign Reveals How Safe Firearm Storage Can Help Prevent Suicide" (September 16, 2020) accessed at https://www.prnewswire.com/news-releases/new-national-campaign-reveals-how-safe-firearm-storage-can-help-prevent-suicide-301132370.html

[13] Ibid.

[14] *Journal of Applied Communication Research*, A. Roberto, G. Meyer, A. Johnson, C. Atkin, P. Smith "Promoting gun trigger-lock use: insights from a radio-based health communication intervention" (January 2011), pp. 210-230, accessed at https://www.tandfonline.com/doi/pdf/10.1080/00909880216584?needAccess=true

[15] Ibid.

[16] FOX 7 Austin, "Safe Gun Storage Saves Lives campaign gives away free gun locks" (March 14, 2022), accessed at https://www.fox7austin.com/news/safe-gun-storage-saves-lives-campaign-free-gun-locks

[17] SAFE GUN STORAGE SAVES LIVES, "Safe Gun Storage Saves Lives" (n.d.), accessed at https://safegunstoragesaveslives.org/

[18] Personal message from Lessa Ross, Director of Lock Arms for Life, November 12, 2022.

[19] BRADY, "New National Campaign Reveals How Safe Firearm Storage Can Help Prevent Suicide" (September 2020), accessed at https://www.bradyunited.org/press-releases/end-family-fire-campaign-suicide-guns

[20] Ibid.

[21] Ibid.

[22] N. Lee, P. Kotler, and J. Colehour, *Social Marketing: Behavior Change for Good,* 7th Ed. (Thousand Oaks, CA: SAGE, 2024), p.83.

[23] Ibid., pp.80-81.

[24] N. Lee, P. Kotler, and J. Colehour, *Social Marketing: Behavior Change for Good,* 7th Ed. (Thousand Oaks, CA: SAGE, 2024)

Chapter 4

Friends
Reaching Out to Someone Who Seems Suicidal

Background, Purpose & Focus

This is the second of three chapters highlighting specific social marketing strategies related to reducing *youth gun suicides*. As noted, it "deserves" three chapters given that suicides accounted for *more than half (54%) of U.S. gun deaths in 2021.*[1] In June of 2022, Everytown Research & Policy, an independent, non-partisan organization dedicated to understanding gun violence, reported that each year more than 3100 young people in the U.S. die by firearm suicide, *an average of nine every day.*[2] "And the problem has only gotten worse. Between 2019 and 2020, the CDC registered a 2 percent increase in the firearm suicide rate. During this same period, the firearm suicide rate among young people ages 10-24 increased 15 percent. And for adolescents ages 10-14, the firearm suicide rate in 2020 was the highest reported by the CDC since 1968 – a 31 percent increase from 2019."[3]

This chapter also briefly highlights the need to reach out to another priority audience, Veterans. As noted in Chapter 1, Veterans represent almost 18% of gun suicides, even though they make up about 7% of the U.S. adult population.[4]

Findings confirm the powerful difference that friends can make when they reach out to someone who seems sad or hopeless. The incidence of this unstable emotional state and vulnerability for suicide is significant among high school youth, as illustrated by findings from CDC's Youth Risk Behavior Surveillance System (YRBSS) that monitors priority health behaviors and attitudes among students across the country, with findings in 2019 relevant to this highlight presented in Table 4.1. In summary, **almost 19% of high school youth have considered attempting suicide in the last year; more than 15% have a plan for how they would attempt suicide; and 9% actually attempted suicide.**

Suicide-Related Attitudes and Behaviors	Total	Female	Male
Felt sad or hopeless (during the 12 months before the survey, almost every day for 2 or more weeks in a row so that they stopped doing some usual activities)	36.7%	46.6%	26.8%
Seriously considered attempting suicide (during the 12 months before the survey)	18.8%	24.1%	13.3%
Made a plan about how they would attempt suicide (during the 12 months before the survey)	15.7%	19.9%	11.3%
Attempted suicide (one of more times during the 12 months before the survey)	8.9%	11.0%	6.6%

Table 4.1 *CDC: High School Youth Risk Behavior Survey, 2019*[5]

Priority Audience & Desired Behavior & Audience Insights

This chapter will highlight efforts to influence *middle school, high school and/or college students who have a friend exhibiting signs that they may be at risk for attempting suicide to reach out and have a conversation.*

Seattle Children's Hospital sites the following common youth suicide warning signs:[6]

- Seeming hopeless about the future
- Exhibiting severe emotional pain or distress
- Having drastic mood and behavior changes
- Engaging in self-harm behaviors
- Talking about or making plans for suicide

Barriers to reaching out and having a conversation about suicide with the friend include the following potential concerns and rationale published by the University of New Hampshire's Psychological & Counseling Services:[7]

- This might "put the idea into their head."
- This might end our friendship.
- My friend might get in trouble.
- Since my friend posted it on social media, there is likely someone else who will step in to help.
- My friend might just be getting back at me for something I did.
- This is probably just something they said because they were drunk.
- They are probably just upset by something, and will be fine once that passes.

A Social Marketing Approach

Forefront Suicide Prevention, a Center of Excellence at the University of Washington, sees most suicides as preventable, and is "on a mission" to support individuals and communities to take action. [8] Core services offered include providing free accessible toolkits (*product, price, place*), with most featuring a consistent framework of five steps to take when faced with supporting someone who may be considering suicide. These **LEARN** steps are provided in a variety of accessible formats for youth who have a friend who seems suicidal including wallet cards, webinars, in person trainings, brochures, and an online toolkit, all highlighting five actions that can be taken, in sequence, to "do something" to prevent a suicide attempt, many that will involve firearms:[9]

1. *Look for Signs:* "Emotions, actions, experiences."
2. *Empathize and Listen*: "Offer compassion, not advice"
3. *Ask Directly About Suicide*: "Are you thinking about suicide?"
4. *Reduce the Dangers*: "Remove or lock up firearms and meds."
5. *Next Steps: Seek Help:* Suicide & Crisis Lifeline: Call or Text 988

Additional efforts for Forefront involve engaging social networks. In 2015, for example, it was announced that Facebook would collaborate with Forefront to enhance its suite of tools to support and influence those who see suicidal posts on Facebook to "help their friend."[10] Based on Forefront's focus on science-based approaches to suicide prevention, Facebook had reached out to Jennifer Stuber, a UW associate professor of social work who started Forefront. Stuber commented in a University of Washington news article that "In the world of suicide prevention, we know that being connected is a protective factor. People are on Facebook 24/7, so there's an opportunity to actually connect a suicidal person with someone they have a relationship with. Facebook is extremely proactive in what they're trying to do."[11] Tools provide concerned friends with suggestions for what to do, offered in a variety of formats including online videos. An employee at Forefront noted in the same news article that he had lost a friend and college classmate to suicide prior to the collaboration, and that he wished had had known that he could have helped. He shared that one night he had "noticed a Facebook post from his friend saying that things were too much, that he couldn't take it anymore."[12] Alarmed, he resolved to call his friend in the morning, but he had died that night. "The thing that breaks my heart the most about this is that I think it was just episodic. I don't think he wanted to die. But I was not trained. I did not know what to do."[13]

Reports in 2022 indicate that Forefront has provided trainings for more than 30,000 health and school professionals and community members in Washington State alone.[14]

Washington State Department of Health

In 2017, the Washington State Department of Health (DOH) worked with social marketing agency C+C to create and launch a youth suicide prevention campaign *Start a Convo, Save a Life*. "The DOH learned from high school students that it's difficult to reach out to friends or classmates who seem depressed, hopeless, or unusually angry to ask them if they are thinking about suicide. The goal of the *Start a Convo, Save a Life* campaign is to help students know that it is okay, even necessary, to start that conversation."[15] The specific purpose of the campaign was to *reduce suicide attempts*, with a focus on a population, *friends of suicidal high school youth*. More specifically, the priority audience within this population was the friend of a classmate who seemed very depressed, hopeless, or unusually angry and said things like:[16]

- "I wish I weren't alive."

- "What's the point of living."
- "Nobody cares about me."

What the campaign was intended to motivate these friends to *do* was inspired by Forefront's LEARN model and included four similar steps:[17]

1. KNOW the warning signs.
2. SHOW you care by asking "What's going on?".
3. ASK the friend "Are you thinking about killing yourself?".
4. CONNECT your friend to a resource for help, or contact them yourself.

A clear *desired benefit* was to "Save the life of a friend."[18] And findings from interviews with students regarding *barriers* were similar to those mentioned earlier from the University of Hampshire's findings:[19]

- It would be awkward.
- It might put the thought in their head, and then they might do it.
- It's too big of a jump.

And what the DOH team learned would be *motivating* included:[20]

- If my friend said, "I wish I weren't alive"
- If someone credible told me, "Asking won't make it more likely they will commit suicide"
- If someone gave me an app that I could use to figure out how to help my friend

A positioning statement inspired by these audience barriers, benefits and motivators was developed by the team: "We want friends of a classmate who seems very depressed, hopeless, or unusually angry, to know it's okay, even necessary, to ask if their friend is thinking of killing themselves and that this courageous act can save the life of their friend."[21]

Several free resources were provided and promoted to "help" get this conversation started. These included a Tumblr site with teen-friendly content about helping a friend, identifying warning signs, providing support, and starting the conversation with someone who may be considering suicide, and also includes campaign creative assets.

Promotional strategies focused on sharing real stories from youth who had helped save the life of a suicidal friend. Overtime, communication channels have included: postings on Facebook and Instagram: posters in hallways and restrooms; special events such as a High School Cafeteria Event where printouts of text messages are posted throughout the cafeteria; and an app encouraging conversations (See Figure 4.1).[22]

Figure 4.1 *Text Message Encouraging a Conversation:* "I really care about you and I'm worried. Can we talk?!?". "Just want it all to go away forever" "This is awkward, but - are u thinking of suicide? Calling u now..."

Source: C+C, A Communications Agency ALL ABOUT THE GOOD

Results

Campaign metrics indicated the Facebook and Instagram components of the campaign resulted in an extremely high click through rate of 5.5 percent, with more than 36,000 impressions and more than 2,000 clicks to the Tumblr site. Almost 60 percent of ad views came from mobile devices. The ads saw a high level of engagement with many commenters tagging friends. The mobile display campaign delivered 3.2 million impressions with more than 5,200 clicks to the campaign website, where a video featuring a friend who had reached out to a suicidal friend achieved an 85 percent completion rate.[23]

Reaching Out To Veterans

The Veterans Administration highlights that "One way to reduce the risk among veterans is to build time and space between a veteran who has expressed thoughts of suicide by firearm."[24] If a person is considering suicide or is at risk of a personal crisis, friends or family members can access the Veterans Crisis Line (988 and select 1) and speak with responders for confidential help. Many of those on the line are Veterans themselves, and the service is private, free, and available 24/7.[25]

Applicable Behavior Change Theories

One of several applicable theories supporting the *Start a Convo. Save a Life.* campaign strategy is the *Social Cognitive Theory*[26] that emphasizes a person needs to believe that the benefits of performing the behavior will outweigh the costs. Significant campaign strategies included success stories from youth who had reached out, helping to ensure others that they too would be likely to save their friend's life. And promotional messages and trusted messengers provided credible information to help reduce concerns that the recommended conversation would make a suicide attempt more likely.

Postings in school cafeterias helped create *injunctive norms*,[27] strengthening student perceptions that having a conversation was "approved" by others in their group.

Social Marketing Principles Contributing To Success[28]

The application of several key social marketing principles were apparent:

- Forefront's partnership model provides a variety of accessible and free customized resources to support a friend to reach out to help (*products, place, and price*).
- The selection of the *priority audience* as "the friend", versus the suicidal student, certainly aligns with a priority audience selection criteria prioritizing those that are "most ready and willing" to do something (e.g., ask), as well as a population that could be identified and reached (e.g., students at a high school, and engaged in social media).
- *Clear, stepwise behaviors* were provided, ones that the app and other resources were designed to address, one a time.
- The perceived likelihood of receiving the *desired benefit* of saving a life was promoted by sharing conversations on social media, as well as real stories such as on videos where the student who was helped expresses their appreciation.

References

[1] Pew Research Center, "What the data says about gun deaths in the U.S." (February 3, 2022), accessed at https://www.pewresearch.org/fact-tank/2022/02/03/what-the-data-says-about-gun-deaths-in-the-u-s/

[2] EVERYTOWN Research & Policy, "The Rise of Firearm Suicide Among Young Americans" (June 2022), accessed at https://everytownresearch.org/report/the-rise-of-firearm-suicide-among-young-americans/

[3] Ibid.

[4] BRADY, "Firearm Suicide Risk Among Veterans and Military Service Members" (2019), accessed at https://www.bradyunited.org/fact-sheets/veterans-and-suicide

[5] CDC "High School YRBS" (2019), accessed at Youth Online: High School YRBS - United States 1991 — 2019 Results I DASH I CDC

[6] Seattle Children's, "Suicide Prevention" (2022), accessed at www.seattlechildrens.org

[7] University of New Hampshire Psychological & Counseling Services, "Helping Your Friends and Peers" (2022), accessed at https://www.unh.edu/pacs/suicide-prevention/helping-your-friends-peers

[8] W "FOREFRONT SUICIDE PREVENTION " (2022), accessed https://in the forefront.org/

[9] W "FOREFRONT SUICIDE PREVENTION" (2022), accessed https://in the forefront.org/learn-saves-lives

[10] UW NEWS, "Forefront and Facebook launch suicide prevention effort" (February 25, 2015), accessed at https://www.washington.edu/news/2015/02/25/forefront-and-facebook-launch-suicide-prevention-effort/

[11] Ibid.

[12] Ibid.

[13] Ibid.

[14] W RESEARCH, "Forefront Suicide Prevention" (2022), accessed at https://www.washington.edu/research/research-centers/forefront-suicide-prevention/

[15] ATHENA, "Start a Convo, Save a Life" Youth Suicide Awareness Campaign Launched" (August 25, 2017), accessed at "Start a Convo, Save a Life" Youth Suicide Awareness Campaign Launched I The Athena Forum

[16] Information provided November 2016, to Nancy Lee by Sigrid Reinert, Suicide Prevention Specialist, Injury & Violence Prevention, Washington State Department of Health.

[17] N. Lee and P. Kotler, *Social Marketing: Behavior Change for Social Good,* 6th Ed. (Thousand Oaks, CA: SAGE PUBLICATIONS, 2020), pp. 79-81.

[18] Information provided November 2016, to Nancy Lee by Sigrid Reinert, Suicide Prevention Specialist, Injury & Violence Prevention, Washington State Department of Health.

[19] N. Lee and P. Kotler, *Social Marketing: Behavior Change for Social Good,* 6th Ed. (Thousand Oaks, CA: SAGE PUBLICATIONS, 2020), pp. 79-81.

[20] Information provided November 2016, to Nancy Lee by Sigrid Reinert, Suicide Prevention Specialist, Injury & Violence Prevention, Washington State Department of Health.

[21] N. Lee and P. Kotler, *Social Marketing: Behavior Change for Social Good,* 6th Ed. (Thousand Oaks, CA: SAGE PUBLICATIONS, 2020), pp. 79-81.

[22] ATHENA, "Start a Convo, Save a Life" Youth Suicide Awareness Campaign Launched" (August 25, 2017), accessed at "Start a Convo, Save a Life" Youth Suicide Awareness Campaign Launched | The Athena Forum

[23] Information provided November 2022, to Nancy Lee by Julie Colehour, C+C.

[24] BRADY, "Firearm Suicide Risk Among Veterans and Military Service Members" (2019), accessed at   https://www.bradyunited.org/fact-sheets/veterans-and-suicide

[25] U.S. Department of Veterans Affairs, "Veteran suicide prevention" (January 2023), accessed at https://www.va.gov/health-care/health-needs-conditions/mental-health/suicide-prevention/

[26] N. Lee, P. Kotler, and J. Colehour, *Social Marketing: Behavior Change for Good,* 7th Ed. (Thousand Oaks, CA: SAGE, 2024), p.83.

[27] N. Lee, P. Kotler, and J. Colehour, *Social Marketing: Behavior Change for Good,* 7th Ed. (Thousand Oaks, CA: SAGE, 2024), p.84.

[28] N. Lee, P. Kotler, and J. Colehour, *Social Marketing: Behavior Change for Good,* 7th Ed. (Thousand Oaks, CA: SAGE, 2024)

Chapter 5

Medical Providers
Helping to Reduce Youth Gun Suicides

Background, Purpose & Focus

The American Academy of Pediatrics (AAP) confirms alarming statistics, some that have been highlighted in other chapters of this book including:[1]

- *An estimated one third of children and youth live in homes with firearms.*
- *Almost half (43%) of these homes contain at least 1 unlocked firearm.*
- *Over 80% of child/youth firearm suicides involved a gun belonging to a family member.*

Relative to other countries, the Council on Injury , Violence and Poison Prevention Executive Committee reported in an AAP publication that: "For youth 5-14 years of age, firearm suicide rates were 8 times higher, and death rates from unintentional firearm injuries were 10 times higher in the United States than other high-income countries. The difference in rates may be related to the ease of availability of guns in the United States compared with other high-income countries."[2]

For more than 30 years, not only has the AAP developed and published statements regarding recommended public policy to address youth gun deaths and injuries, but they have also supported a social marketing approach, one influencing medical providers to contribute to a purpose of *reducing youth gun suicides*, with a focus on *universal screenings*. They affirm this direction with important relevant findings:

- Most young people keep suicidal thoughts to themselves, and therefore may not mention this unless they are asked a direct question. [3]
- Universal screening is different than "targeted screening" which most often relates to screening only behavioral health patients for suicide risk.[4]
- Universal screening can also help address equity issues, by ensuring all youth are screened for suicide risk across demographic groups, communities, and care settings.[5]
- Research shows that most people who die by suicide have visited a healthcare provider in the weeks or months before their death and that asking about suicide risk can be a way to recognize someone at risk and get them help, as well as ensure guns in their homes are safety secured.[6]
- Physician counseling of parents about firearm safety appears to be effective.[7]

A Social Marketing Approach

Priority Audience & Desired Behavior

AAP efforts prioritize *pediatricians with patients 12 and older*, and are intended to influence them to *conduct the uniquely defined universal screenings*. This screening is for patients who have no history of suicide risk, and is recommended to be conducted no more than once a month and no less than once a year. When findings indicate the patient is at risk for suicide, several next steps including having discussions with family members regarding safe gun storage, and tools and resources to facilitate the discussion process are provided.

Audience Insights & Objectives

Key knowledge and belief objectives AAP notes that help address barriers, desired benefits, as well as potential motivators for medical providers to do these universal screenings include :[8]

- Although many are concerned with "putting the idea into their heads", studies have found no longitudinal changes in suicidal ideation that are associated with assessing for suicide risk.
- Support among pediatricians for screening to prevent gun deaths and injuries is strong, with surveys indicating that 95% of AAP members agree that pediatricians should ask parents with firearms to unload and lock them away.

In addition, programs and resources need to address common likely concerns with the amount of time the screenings will add to the appointment, as well as concern with patient and parent desire for privacy.

Key Strategies

AAP offers a variety of free universal screening tools (*product and price*) for medical providers, ones related to assessing suicide risk as well as safe firearm storage. Access to tools (*place*) is provided on websites offering resources for more information and standards of practice including:[9]

- A list of screening questions tailored to types of clinical practices. An article in the Psychiatric Times shared the following 4 questions, ones especially relevant to parents of children/youth:[10]

  1. "Do you have access to firearms?
  2. Why do you own them?

3. How do you store them?
4. Do you understand the suicide risk firearms pose?"

- Ways to integrate the screening into other preventive service screeners and questionnaires, as well as clinical workflow or electronic health records to ease implementation
- Options for conducting screenings via conversations, via paper-and-pencil, or on electronic tablet
- Identifying what members of the clinical team can administer the screening, including, in many cases, those who are already taking health history early in the visit, such as a nurse or medical assistant
- Importance of using trained interpreters for those with limited English proficiency
- Recommendations to screen patients without a parent/caregiver in the room to encourage open and honest discussion
- Frequency of at least once a year

Tools specifically related to support providers in promoting safe firearm storage to their patients include:[11]

o A *video* series "Safer: Storing Firearms Prevents Harm"
o A *course* "Safer: Storing Firearms Prevents Harm Course", designed to support providers to effectively counsel patient families
o A *course* "CALM for Pediatric Providers" focusing on how to have conversations that lead to safer outcomes for youth
o *Podcasts and Blogs* including "Firearm Injuries during the Pandemic", "Common Sense Ways Pediatricians Can Help Reduce Firearm Injuries, and "Why Should Pediatricians Ask about Guns in the Home"

In addition to the brief physician screening and counseling for parents, AAP encourages providers to give parents informational brochures containing motivating statistics and instructions for safe storage, as well as access to any local programs such as those offered by police departments that offer discounted or free safety devices such as trigger locks, lock boxes and gun safes.

Promotional strategies often supported by AAP include messages likely to increase provider motivation, as well as parental understanding for having the conversation. Messages suggested by Dr. Michael P. Hirsh on an AAP Voices Blog are examples of ones to motivate providers to have the conversation, as well as increase likelihood that parents will follow up after their visit with safe gun storage practices :

- "For pediatricians, asking parents about guns in the home – and whether they are properly stored – shouldn't be any different than asking about the use of car seats, smoke alarms, bike helmets and other safety measures."[12]
- "If a parent replies 'yes' to gun ownership, ask about their storage practices."[13]
- "You encourage parents to ask if there might be peanuts in their friend's household if your patient has a peanut allergy. The question about access to firearms should be as seamless."[14]
- Share with parents the statistic that "Roughly 80% of unintentional firearm deaths of kids under age 15 occur in a home."[15]

Results

Overall, AAP reports that "in controlled studies, individuals who received physician counseling were more likely to report the adoption of 1 or more safe gun-storage practices."[16]

One example is that of an evidence-based pediatric care primary care program, *Safety Check,* delivered by pediatricians and informed by a screening and counseling approach to reduce firearm injuries. A large clinical trial evaluated outcomes of the program compared to a control group. The program, delivered by pediatricians, included:

- Screening for the presence of firearms, firearm storage, and parental concerns about firearm injuries where children live and/or play
- Counseling using brief motivational interviewing
- Providing firearm safe storage tools such a cable lock

The clinical trial found that parents who received the *Safety Check* intervention doubled the odds of safe firearm storage compared to the control group. The group receiving the intervention showed a 10% increase in parent-reported use of cable locks, while there was a 12% decrease in cable locks in a control group. And follow up research paved the way for adaptations including expanding the reach to a broader range (e.g., from 2-11 year olds to 5-17 year olds), to incorporating the screening as a universal screening tool versus a separate conversation, and offering additional resources from trusted and accessible sources such as brochures or website links. Based on crowd-sourced feedback from parents, the program name was changed to S.A.F.E. *Firearm* (Suicide and Accident Prevention through Family Education). [17]

Applicable Behavior Change Theories

Several components of the *Health Belief Model* confirm key intervention strategies used to influence medical providers to conduct these universal screenings, and to then have discussions with parents regarding safe gun storage practices:[18]

Perceived Susceptibility: As noted earlier, AAP highlights persuasive statistics such as the fact that an estimated 80% of child/youth firearm suicides involved a gun belonging to a family member, and that most young people keep suicidal thoughts to themselves and may not bring up the topic on their own if they aren't asked a direct question.

Cues to Action: Likelihood of providers asking questions of parents regarding safe gun storage are likely to occur automatically given the universal screenings which are intended to occur at least annually.

The Theory of Reasoned Action[19] suggests that an intention to adopt a desired behavior is likely to be influenced by how the audience perceives the behavior among "important others", in this case AAP. Providers are certainly likely to perceive this as an approved practice, and one they are supported to perform successfully. Further, the related *Theory of Planned Behavior*[20] points to the "power of habit" to influence action, in this case as a result of universal screening.

Relevant theories related to *Social Norms*[21] are also applicable, including:

Injunctive Norms, given the AAP recommends and promotes that universal screenings to include questions related to risk of suicide, as well as subsequent discussions with parents regarding safe storage.

Personal Norms, illustrated by the likelihood that providers having the discussion with the parents of a patient who may be at risk for suicide would be seen as consistent with their standards of practice.

Social Marketing Principles Contributing to Success[22]

The application of several key social marketing principles were apparent in this chapter's featured efforts:

- *Address Audience Barriers*: AAP highlights persuasive statistics such as ones regarding the need for safe gun storage; addresses concerns about increasing the likelihood of suicide; and provides resources such as tips on how to have comfortable and instructive conversations with parents.
- *Use Trusted Messengers*: Certainly, AAP has credibility with the providers. For parents, also an audience to be influenced, their child' healthcare provider is a credible resource for health and injury prevention practices.
- *Ensure Diversity, Equity, and Inclusion*: The shift of recommended practice from targeted screenings to universal screenings helps to address a concern expressed in a study by scientists at Northwestern Medicine, the University of Pennsylvania, Henry Ford Health, and Kaiser Permanente Colorado. They found that secure storage programs when implemented are successful, but may not be reaching all parents equitably. "In the new study, scientists examined a well-established firearm violence-prevention program offered to parents of children ages 5 to 17 during routine pediatric checkups is often not offered to parents of girls and some racial and ethnic minorities."[23]

References

[1] American Academy of Pediatrics, "Gun Safety and Injury Prevention" (July 27, 2022), https://www.aap.org/en/patient-care/gun-safety-and-injury-prevention/

[2] American Academy of Pediatrics, "Firearm-Related Injuries Affecting the Pediatric Population" (November 1, 2012), https://publications.aap.org/pediatrics/article/130/5/e1416/32375/Firearm-Related-Injuries-Affecting-the-Pediatric?

[3] American Academy of Pediatrics, "Screening for Suicide Risk in Clinical Practice" (February 14, 2022) , https://www.aap.org/en/patient-care/blue print-for-youth-suicide-prevention/strategies-for-clinical-settings-for-youth-suicide-prevention/screening-for-suicide-risk-in-clinical-practice/

[4] Ibid.

[5] Ibid.

[6] Ibid.

[7] American Academy of Pediatrics, "Firearm-Related Injuries Affecting the Pediatric Population" (November 1, 2012), https://publications.aap.org/pediatrics/article/130/5/e1416/32375/Firearm-Related-Injuries-Affecting-the-Pediatric?

[8] American Academy of Pediatrics, "Screening for Suicide Risk in Clinical Practice" (February 14, 2022) , https://www.aap.org/en/patient-care/blue print-for-youth-suicide-prevention/strategies-for-clinical-settings-for-youth -suicide-prevention/screening-for-suicide-risk-in-clinical-practice. And https://www.aap.org/en/patient-care/gun-safety-and-injury-prevention/

[9] Ibid.

[10] *Psychiatric Times,* "How to talk to patients about firearms", (May 2021), T. Thrasher, accessed at https://www.psychiatrictimes.com/view/how-to-talk-to-patients-about-firearms

[11] American Academy of Pediatrics, "Gun Safety and Injury Prevention" (July 27, 2022), https://www.aap.org/en/patient-care/gun-safety-and-injury-prevention/

[12] American Academy of Pediatrics, Hirsh, M. Blog, "Common Sense Ways Pediatricians Can Help Reduce Firearm Injuries" (June 12 2019) AAP 5 Common Sense Ways Pediatricians Can Help Reduce Firearm Injuries (aap.org)

[13] Ibid.

[14] Ibid.

[15] Ibid.

[16] American Academy of Pediatrics, "Gun Safety and Injury Prevention" (July 27, 2022), https://www.aap.org/en/patient-care/gun-safety-and-injury-prevention/

[17] BMC, Beidas et al., "Study protocol for a type III hybrid effectiveness-implementation trial of strategies to implement firearm safety promotion as a universal suicide prevention strategy in pediatric primary care" (2021), https://implementationscience.biomedcentral.com/articles/10.1186/s13012-021-01154-8

[18] N. Lee, P. Kotler, and J. Colehour, *Social Marketing: Behavior Change for Good,* 7th Ed. (Thousand Oaks, CA: SAGE, 2024), p.80-81.

[19] Ibid., pp.82-83.

[20] Ibid.

[21] Ibid., pp.84-86.

[22] N. Lee, P. Kotler, and J. Colehour, *Social Marketing: Behavior Change for Good,* 7th Ed. (Thousand Oaks, CA: SAGE, 2024)

[23] University of Pennsylvania, "Northwestern Now: Safe gun storage programs are successful – if implemented" (October 19, 2022), accessed at Northwestern Now: Safe Gun Storage Programs Are Successful — If Implemented - Center for Health Incentives and Behavioral Economics (upenn.edu)

Chapter 6

Upstanders
"Say Something" to Report Warning Signs of a School Shooting

Background: Sandy Hook Elementary School Shooting

On December 14, 2012, shortly after 9:30 a.m. in Newtown, Connecticut, a 20-year-old male shot and killed 26 people at the Sandy Hook Elementary school using his mother's AR-15 as his primary weapon.[1] An estimated 154 shots were fired.[2] Twenty of the victims were children between six and seven years old in the first grade. Six were adult staff members at the school including the school's principal, two teachers, a special education aide, a behavior therapist, and a school psychologist.[3] School staff called 911 at about 9:35 a.m., and first responders arrived at the school within minutes and shortly thereafter found the shooter dead from a self-inflicted gunshot wound.

Sometime that morning before coming to the school, the gunman shot and killed his mother at their Newtown home. At the time of this incident, this was one of the deadliest school shooting in U.S. history.[4]

Under Connecticut law at the time, the shooter was old enough to carry a long gun, such as a rifle or shotgun, but too young to own or carry handguns, and the guns he used had been purchased legally by his mother, with whom there was currently a strained relationship.[5] Relevant subsequent reports about the shooter provided information about his profile and potential motives:

- The Connecticut State's Attorney's office concluded that the shooter acted alone and had planned his actions.[6]
- A report from the Office of Child Advocate highlighted that he had Asperger syndrome and as a teenager had depression, anxiety, and obsessive-compulsive disorder, but concluded that this had not caused or led to his murderous acts. Instead, his severe and deteriorating internalized mental health problems ... combined with an atypical preoccupation with violence ... and access to deadly weapons ... proved a recipe for mass murder."[7]
- A former teacher described him as exhibiting antisocial behavior, rarely interacting with other students, and obsessed with writing "about battles, destruction and war."[8]
- The State Attorney concluded in a final report in 2013 that the gunman "had familiarity with and access to firearms and ammunition and an obsession with mass murders, in particular the April 1999 shootings at Columbine High School in Colorado."[9]

A report from the Office of Child Advocate in Connecticut noted that all along the way there were "red flags" signifying disaster and "significant failures of the educational and mental health systems to coordinate their efforts to compose and enact a thoroughgoing, comprehensive set of interventions ... And despite his deteriorating condition, he had unfettered access to the guns. He participated in chatrooms dealing with mass murder and an online gaming *Call of Duty* and *School Shooter*." [10]

Policy & Legislative Response[11]

Following the Sandy Hook massacre, in 2013 proponents of gun control proposed federal legislation - an Assault Weapons Ban, one that would prohibit the sale of more than 150 specific firearm models as well as magazines that held more than 10 rounds of ammunition. Although there was widespread public support for the bill, it was defeated 60-40 in the Senate. Another proposed bill would have mandated criminal background checks for firearm sales over the Internet, but was also rejected by the Senate.

A Social Marketing Approach

Purpose & Focus

In January of 2013, many of the families and loved ones of some of those who were killed or injured in the attack gathered to form *Sandy Hook Promise*, a national, non-profit organization based in Newtown, Connecticut. Their overall purpose and focus was no doubt inspired by the facts shared on the Sandy Hook Promise website that *"93% of school shooters planned the attack in advance"* [12] and *"in 4 out of 5 school shootings, at least one other person had knowledge of the attacker's plan but failed to report it."*[13]

Sandy Hook Promise *"**envisions** a future where all children are free from school shootings and other acts of violence"*, and is on a **mission** "to educate and empower youth and adults to prevent violence in schools, homes, and communities."[14]

Using a social marketing framework, this case example represents one with a purpose to *reduce school shootings* with a focus on *"safely and anonymously reporting potential threats before they happen."* [15]

Priority Audiences & Desired Behaviors

Overall, intervention efforts have been developed to engage and influence priority audiences that can head off acts of violence at schools and in communities, and include Middle & High School students, teachers, counselors, and parents. As noted in Chapter 1, a majority of school shooters are reported as being male (95%) and white (61%).[16]

The *Know the Signs* programs launched 18 months after the founding of Sandy Hook Promise. Behavior objectives focus on priority audiences **knowing** *the warning signs that someone is at-risk of hurting themselves or others, act immediately by telling something to a trusted adult or use an anonymous reporting system to get help.* A summary of ten critical warning signs of violence posted on the Sandy Hook Promise website include:[17]

1. Withdrawing from friends, family, and usual activities
2. Bullying others
3. Being excessively irritable
4. Experiencing chronic loneliness or social isolation
5. Expressing persistent thoughts of harming themselves or others
6. Making direct threats toward people or places
7. Bragging about having access to guns or weapons
8. Recruiting others to engage or be an audience for an attack
9. Expressing a planned threat
10. Exhibiting cruelty to animals

Audience Insights

Major concerns for students to "intervene", and/or report on a fellow student's behavior, would understandably include concerns about whether or not the warning signs they noticed were relevant or significant; what they should say, if anything to the student; to whom, when and how they should express their concerns; and, perhaps most significantly, would they get retribution from the troubled youth if they "told someone."

Many of these concerns are similar for teachers, counselors, and parents, needing more clarity and specificity of the warning signs; knowing whether or not the next best step is to approach the troubled youth; and what resources to access to help the youth and how.

Key Strategies

For Students

Three major Sandy Hook Promise programs designed to influence and support students to take action include:[18]

- *Start With Hello* for grades K-12 empowers students to recognize loneliness and social isolation in their peers, and then presents effective ways to reach out and help. Additional benefits highlighted include how their efforts can help grow empathetic and inclusive communities.
- *Say Something,* also for grades K-12, is designed to achieve three goals: 1) Recognize warning signs and threats of a Classmate who may be-at-risk of hurting themselves or others; 2) Say something to a Trusted Adult to get help; 3) Grow a community of Upstanders who look out for one another.
- *SAVE Promise Clubs* are student-led organizations and embed the teachings of *Say Something* and *Start With Hello* within the school community.
- *Say Something Anonymous Reporting System* for grades 4-12 also teaches students how to recognize warning signs and threats of someone who may be at-risk of hurting themselves

or others. What this program provides, uniquely, is the ability to report anonymously using a downloadable app, telephone hotline or website (See Figure 6.1). The program is directed by a former educator/administrator. Messages are received by trained crisis counselors, fluent in multiple languages, trained in suicide prevention, crisis management, and mental health support. The system enables students to anonymously report an issue 24/7/365. A list of issues comes up with more than 30 options including ones for Planned School Attack, "Intent to Harm someone", Gang Violence, Suicide/Suicide Ideation. Tips are uploaded with secure intel to a live 24/7 crisis center where all tips reported are managed until the cases are resolved.

Figure 6.1 *Say Something Downloadable App.*

Source: Sandy Hook Promise

For Teachers & Educators[19]

For teachers and educators, Sandy Hook Promise developed an accessible Online Virtual Learning Center, designed by educators, and informed by research. Everything on the Learning Center is available at no cost and includes training videos, interactive lessons, school safety lesson plans, and a searchable digital library of resources. Asynchronous training is available from phones, tablets or desktop devices, and educators and parents can access the platform for free. Registration is intended to be simple, by just providing an email address. Materials available include school safety lesson plans, violence prevention worksheets, and a newsletter to learn about opportunities to connect with other educators, sharing best practices and learning.

For Parents

Educator's Online Virtual Learning materials and anonymous reporting systems are also available to parents, as well as workshops on Being a Trusted Adult.

Results

As of July 2023, the following outcomes and impact were reported on the Sandy Hook Promise website, https://www.sandyhook promise.org/who-we-are/our-impact

- 185,000+ *anonymous tips* have been received
- 493 *lives* have been confirmed as saved
- 15 *planned school shootings* have been prevented
- 184 *acts of violence with a weapon* have been prevented
- 9+ million people have made the *promise* to protect children from gun violence
- 21,000 individuals have participated in the *Know the Signs* Program trainings

In September of 2022, an example of the value of the program was captured in a quote from a school district Director of Student Services in California: "We had a student that was contemplating suicide and several friends reported it online on the Say Something app ... Sandy Hook Promise, a national group advocating for school safety, is funding this app that we're learning has already saved the lives of six students ... 39 days in, we received 42 tips so far ... eight tips where the police department went out to the home to interview the student and six were life-saving tips, so we could directly intervene in the students' life." [20]

Applicable Behavior Change Theories

Participation in the programs has likely been influenced, in part, by *personal norms*, in this case with participants engaging in the program as it is seen to be consistent with personal values and standards they have for their individual behaviors. Additionally, *injunctive norms* are also a likely influence, with behaviors adopted out of perceiving them as being "approved by others in the individual's group."[21]

The program reflects application of several components of the *Community-Based Prevention Model*, [22] where interventions are designed and led, in large part, by community members, a strategy often more likely to succeed than ones planned and executed by "outsiders." Social marketers collaborate with community members to critically analyze community problems, and develop implement interventions based on audience insights.

Social Marketing Principles Contributing to Success[23]

Application of several social marketing principles contributed to the program's success:

- The *priority audience,* students of a peer exhibiting signs of potential violence, was one seen as most likely to adopt a behavior change that would have the most impact on the "wicked problem."
- *Clear, specific behaviors* were determined and promoted including knowing the warning signs and sharing concerns with a trusted resource.
- Multiple programs (products) were developed to *remove major barriers* to "saying something", especially the anonymous tip app that not only makes the students feel safe, put also provided a familiar and popular resource for outreach.
- The programs were *accessible and free.*
- Personal and visible *pledges/commitment* interventions were incorporated to sustain behaviors, as well as strengthen perceived norms.
- Program engagement, outcomes and impact *are monitored and reported* on.

References

1 Britannica Online Encyclopedia, "Sandy Hook Elementary School Shooting", (August 12, 2022), https://www.britannica.com/event/Sandy-Hook-Elementary-School-shooting

2 Ibid.

3 Ibid.

4 Ibid.

5 Wikipedia, "Sandy Hook Elementary School Shooting" (July 2023), accessed at https://en.wikipedia.org/wiki/Sandy_Hook_Elementary_School_shooting#cite_note-cga-28Ibid .

6 "Sandy Hook report – shooter Adam Lanza was obsessed with mass murder". The Guardian. November 25, 2013. Archived from the original on November 26, 2013. Retrieved November 26, 2013.

7 Office of the Child Advocate, State of Connecticut, "Shooting at Sandy Hook Elementary School", p.9, section 36 (November 21, 2014), http://www.ct.gov/oca/lib/oca/sandyhook11212014.pdf and CNN, "Report finds missed chances to help Newtown shooter Adam Lanza" (November 2014), accessed at https://www.cnn.com/2014/11/21/justice/newtown-shooter-adam-lanza-report/index.html

8 "Police file on Newtown yields chilling portrait". The Washington Post. Associated Press. December 27, 2013. Archived from the original on December 13, 2015. Retrieved December 28, 2013.

9 "Sandy Hook report – shooter Adam Lanza was obsessed with mass murder". The Guardian. November 25, 2013. Archived from the original on November 26, 2013..

10 The Psychology Times, "Reflections on Sandy Hook", author Dr. Yael Banai, https://thepsychologytimes.com/2016/03/17/reflections-on-sandy-hook/

11 Britannica Online Encyclopedia, "Sandy Hook Elementary School Shooting", (August 12, 2022), https://www.britannica.com/event/Sandy-Hook-Elementary-School-shooting

12 Sandy Hook Promise, "17 Facts About Gun Violence and School Shootings" (2023), accessed at https://www.sandyhookpromise.org/blog/gun-violence/facts-about-gun-violence-and-school-shootings/

13 Ibid.

14 Sandy Hook Promise, "Our Mission" (2022), https://www.sandyhookpromise.org/who-we-are/about-us/

15 Sandy Hook Promise, "Say Something Anonymous Reporting System" (2023), accessed at Say Something Anonymous Reporting System — Sandy Hook Promise

16 BROOKINGS, "School shootings: What we know about them, and what we can do to prevent them" (January 2022), R. Kowalski, accessed at https://www.brookings.edu/blog/brown-center-chalkboard/2022/01/26/school-shootings-what-we-know-about-them-and-what-we-can-do-to-prevent-them/

17 Sandy Hook Promise, "10 Critical Warning Signs of Violence" (2022), https://www.sandyhookpromise.org/who-we-are/about-us

18 Sandy Hook Promise, "Learning Center" (2022), https://www.sandyhookpromiselearning.org

19 Sandy Hook Promise, "What's Available on the Learning Center?" (2022), https://www.sandyhookpromise.org/our-programs/program-overview/online-virtual-learning-for-bullying-violence-and-suicide-prevention/

20 Fox News, "Say Something app for students addresses suicide, violence and concerns" (September 26, 2019), https://www.ktvu.com/news/say-something-app-for-students-addresses-suicide-violence-and-safety-concerns

21 N. Lee, P. Kotler, and J. Colehour, *Social Marketing: Behavior Change for Good*, 7th Ed. (Thousand Oaks, CA: SAGE, 2024), pp.84-85.

22 Ibid., pp.101-102.

23 N. Lee, P. Kotler, and J. Colehour, *Social Marketing: Behavior Change for Good*, 7th Ed. (Thousand Oaks, CA: SAGE, 2024)

Chapter 7

School Threat Assessment Teams
Identifying & Intervening With Potential Shooters

Background

While it is reported there are hundreds of shootings that have taken place at schools across the U.S. in the past 20 years, as of 2019, there were 11 classified as *mass shootings*, defined by the FBI as "an incident in which four or more victims, not including the suspect, are killed."[1] Some of the most memorable of these to many were the mass school shootings at Columbine High School in Oklahoma in 1999, Sandy Hook Elementary School in Connecticut in 2012, and Marjory Stoneman Douglas High School in Parkland, Florida, in 2018. This chapter demonstrates how School Threat Assessment Teams (STAT) can help reduce incidents such as these, saving lives and reducing injuries that might have occurred had they been carried out.

The U.S. Department of Education describes School Threat Assessment Teams (STAT) as "a group of officials that convene to identify, evaluate, and address threats or potential threats to school security. Threat assessment teams review incidents of threatening behavior reported by students (current and former), parents, school employees, or other individuals."[2] Members of a threat assessment team include officials who can assist in making decisions regarding the need for and type of intervention, and most often include school principals, counselors, school law enforcement officials, as well as outside medical and mental health professionals, and local law enforcement officers.

This chapter highlights one STAT program, The Mid-Valley Student Threat Assessment Team, formed in 2000 in the state of Oregon, one of the first collaborations of its kind.[3] As you will read, school threat assessment teams are considered a social marketing approach, as the team engages in persuading a student who may intend to carry out an act of violence to accept help and support that then decreases the risk of a school shooting being carried out. Relative to the social marketing framework, this is an example of a midstream audience (the team) empowered to influence a downstream audience (potential shooter).

A Social Marketing Approach

Purpose & Focus

The Mid-Valley Student Threat Assessment Team intends to *"prevent school shootings from happening in the first place."*[4] The program structure focuses on *recognizing and then reporting on communications by a student that imply an intent to harm other people.* It relies on this being reported most often by other students, school staff, and/or community partners. Threatening communications may be in a variety of forms including verbal conversations and written messages, especially on social media. In addition to reporting on apparent intents to harm others, other red flags include a student's unusual interest in prior school shootings, violence, and/or a preoccupation with weapons. Once reported, threat assessment teams are trained to take impactful next steps.

Priority Audiences & Desired Behaviors

The Mid-Valley Student Threat Assessment Team is administered by a collaborative team comprised of school employees including school counselors, teachers, and principals, as well as community law enforcement officials, and public mental health professionals. When an incident is reported, teams have been trained to meet and engage in a series of sequential acts:[5]

- **Gather more information** about the situation reported, including talking with parents and other school-based staff who might be aware of the concerning communications/red flags. Questions asked of parents include whether the student has access to weapons.
- **Determine the level of concern** for the reported incident, using standard protocols to assess risk factors.
- If the situation is threatening, **determine what kind of support** should be provided to the student of concern.
- **Organize resources and a plan to provide recommended support**, which may include bringing in public mental health or law enforcement, as well as those working at youth serving agencies in the community.
- **Plan implementation** commonly includes efforts such as the following:
    o School staff, or other team members, meet with the student and share the team's concerns that have been noted; highlight the intent to support them; help them understand the consequences of their potential violent action; and ensure the student "that people will help them to move in a positive direction."[6]
    o Law enforcement goes to the student's home and talks to parents about whether there is access to weapons and the importance of securing them.

Audience Insights

An interview by Dave Miller on Oregon Public Broadcasting (OPB) with Courtenay McCarthy, a school based psychologist at the Salem-Keizer school district in Oregon and a STAT team leader, was published by OPB in June of 2022, and included perspectives on barriers and benefits related to team members taking some of the recommended actions, especially one-on-one conversations with parents and students.[7]

Insights discussed in the interview regarding having conversations with *students* include:

- It is surprising to many that students are actually comfortable sharing what's going on in their life, providing the team with insights on how to assist them.
- When this isn't the case, it is important to engage other sources close to the student including classmates and teachers.
- Kids that are at risk for extreme aggression such as shootings often don't have close, trusting relationships with adults, and connecting them with people in school settings and community partners can help them understand they have someone who can stand up for them and help them.

Insights regarding conversations with *parents* include:

- It is not uncommon that parents may initially push back when hearing about the concerns.
- Providing parents with detailed information that has been discovered, and concerns that have been revealed, will assist in having "the full picture", increasing acceptance of support to take important next steps to prevent their child from taking the concerned violent actions.

- Engaging law enforcement in conversations with the parents is likely to help increase cooperation with protective next steps.

Additional relevant perspectives shared in the interview that support these conversations, and other relevant interventions, included:[8]

- An alternative action, that of removing a student from the school, can have negative impacts, potentially increasing the student's grievance, motivating them to take the violent actions they had been pondering.
- Youth with the potential for extreme aggression are often those who don't have close and trusting relationships with adults, and creating those relationships within the school setting and with community partners can fill this void and provide hope.

Key Strategies & Results

Mark Follman, in his book *TRIGGER POINTS: Inside the Million to Stop Mass Shootings in America,* published in 2022, describes the formation, structure and impact of the Salem-Keizer School District's Mid-Valley Student Threat Assessment Team, one that is present in the district's sixty-five school facilities. [9] Salem-Keizer's roughly 240 administrators and 100 counselors received program **trainings**, ones described by a lead founder of STAT, John Van Dreal, as being efficient and user-friendly.[10] "It's a pretty simple process: When a case comes up, you work together to figure out more specifically what's worrying you, and you make a plan to intervene. Then you meet again and follow up on the plan."[11] Trainings include sharing case stories of student interventions, and then detail on team responses. Follman further reported that the Salem-Keizer district had seen about 250 new cases at the building level each year, among which 55 cases each year were elevated to the STAT experts for assistance. "Among those, a handful proved particularly serious, rated by the team as moderate or occasionally high risk for targeted violence."[12]

One incident noted in Follman's book that Courteney McCarthy shared involved a student reporting that while waiting at a school bus stop she had heard a classmate saying:

> "Don't come to school this Friday. I'm coming back here with my dad's semiautomatic and shooting up the place."[13]

The school's threat assessment process was engaged by the team, and included law enforcement going to the student's home and talking with the parents as well as the student. Parents were supported to involve the student in mental health counseling. McCarthy shared that "with all those processes in place to support him, he ended up doing better, and he ended up graduating from high school, and by all accounts, he seems to be doing well at this point."[14]

Dissemination

The National Center for Education Statistics reported in 2018 that 42% of public schools reported having a threat assessment team during the 2015-2016 school year, and the team was defined as "a formalized group of persons who meet on a regular basis with the common purpose of identifying, assessing, and managing students who may pose a threat of targeted violence in schools"; and that "school-based assessment teams are usually some combination of school administrators, teachers, counselors, sworn law enforcement officers, and mental health professionals."[15] A higher percentage of high schools (52%) have teams than do middle schools (45%) and primary schools (39%). More than a third (36%) of the teams indicate meeting at least once a month to discuss a current threat.[16]

And, as of October of 2022, while most states do not have a specific law mandating the creation of these teams, many schools have adopted the measure in order to protect their students.[17]

As an example of diffusion in one state, Virginia, "during the 2017-18 school year, 80% of K-12 public schools reported conducting at least one threat assessment. Overall, schools reported a total of 14,869 threat assessments. Of these cases, 1,472, or about 10%, reached the highest threat level classification at some point in the threat assessment process."[18] Data analysis indicated that "less than 1% of the 14,869 reported threats actually resulted in a related act being carried out. In total, school officials reported that only 42 of our threat assessment cases included an event taking place, such as a student attempting to harm themselves or others. We believe that's a pretty good success rate for our teams." [19]

Applicable Behavior Change Theories

One model that mirrors the establishment process and uptake for STAT programs is *Community-Based Prevention Marketing*[20] which is applicable when interventions are designed and directed by community members. Relevant to this case highlight, the framework development for the assessments and subsequent support included representatives from school staff, law enforcement, and local youth services collaborating to conduct assessments and develop supportive strategies.

In terms of building and leveraging social norms, one of the most applicable for this model is the *Explicit Norm*[21] model which refers to norms that are created by being *written and openly expressed*, as are the clear actions for STAT members, including incident tracking, frequency of meetings, and outcomes.

Social Marketing Principles Contributing to Success[22]

Several social marketing principles for success are evident in the framework:

- The priority audience for this case is an influential *midstream audience,* a credible and trustworthy team of professionals supported to take the next step (behavior) when an *"upstander" reports a potential harmful incident.*
- Guidelines for the teams supported a *Behavior Chain* approach, beginning with the awareness of a potential violent behavior, risk assessment with established protocols, activating resources to help, and then providing sustainable support.
- A clear *product* that helps the team is the accessibility of trainings for the team members, providing a coordinated, efficient, and proven structural approach. Programs lacking this structure don't often benefit from this community approach.

References

[1] ABC News, "The 11 mass deadly school shootings that happened since Columbine" (April 19, 2019), accessed at https://abcnews.go.com/US/11-mass-deadly-school-shootings-happened-columbine/story?id=62494128

[2] U.S. Department of Education, "What is a threat assessment team?" (n.d.), accessed at https://studentprivacy.ed.gov/faq/what-threat-assessment-team

[3] Student Threat Assessment, "Mid-Valley Threat Assessment system" (n.d.), accessed at (https://sites.google.com/a/salemkeizer.net/student-threat-assessment/student-threat-assessment-system

[4] Sheraz Adiq (OPB), "Oregon school district pioneered a system to prevent school shootings" (June 9, 2022), accessed at https://www.opb.org/article/2022/06/01/oregon-school-district-pioneered-a-system-to-prevent-school-shootings/

[5] Ibid.

[6] Ibid.

[7] Ibid.

[8] Ibid.

[9] M. Follman, *Trigger Points: Inside the Mission to Stop Mass Shootings in America* (HarperCollins, 2022), pp.109-138.

[10] Ibid., p.111

[11] Ibid., p.112.

[12] Ibid., p.113.

[13] Ibid.

[14] Sheraz Adiq (OPB), "Oregon school district pioneered a system to prevent school shootings" (June 9, 2022), accessed at https://www.opb.org/article/2022/06/01/oregon-school-district-pioneered-a-system-to-prevent-school-shootings/

[15] NCES, "What Are Threat Assessment Teams and How Prevalent Are They in Public Schools?" (July 10, 2018), accessed at https://nces.ed.gov/blogs/nces/post/what-are-threat-assessment-teams-and-how-prevalent-are-they-in-public-schools

[16] Ibid.

[17] The Blackwell Firm, "School Threat Assessment Teams: Keeping Students Safe" (November 24, 2022), accessed at https://theblackwellfirm.com/school-threat-assessment-teams-keeping-students-safe/

[18] National Institute of Justice, "The Value of Threat Assessment Teams" (November 2019), accessed at https://nij.ojp.gov/topics/articles/value-threat-assessment-teams

[19] Ibid.

[20] N. Lee, P. Kotler, and J. Colehour, *Social Marketing: Behavior Change for Good,* 7th Ed. (Thousand Oaks, CA: SAGE, 2020), p.90.

[21] N. Lee, P. Kotler, and J. Colehour, *Social Marketing: Behavior Change for Good,* 7th Ed. (Thousand Oaks, CA: SAGE, 2024), p.84.

[22] N. Lee, P. Kotler, and J. Colehour, *Social Marketing: Behavior Change for Good,* 7th Ed. (Thousand Oaks, CA: SAGE, 2024)

Chapter 8

Heroic Bystanders
Becoming First Responders

Background

From 2015-2019, there were nearly *400 mass shooting incidents per year, more than 1 a day on average.*[1] As noted in Chapter 1, most statistics presented in this book will be for those prior to 2020, given the impact of COVID. For this chapter's background section, however, 2022 data is summarized, providing an update on incidents where more detailed information was available. The Year 2022 was the highest year on record for mass shootings in the U.S. Based on data compiled by the Gun Violence Archive, a non-profit that tracks gun violence incidents across the country, as of December 20, 2022, there were 647 mass shootings almost two per day on average.[2] Those incidents with the highest total number of injuries and deaths included 15 that are briefly described in Table 8.1:[3]

Date (2022)	Total # Deaths & Injuries	City & State	Setting/Location
February 19	16	Charleston, Missouri	Abandoned Building
February 26	14	Las Vegas, Nevada	Hookah Lounge
March 19	27	Dumas, Arkansas	Car Show
April 3	16	Dallas, Texas	Concert

Date (2022)	Total # Deaths & Injuries	City & State	Setting/Location
April 3	18	Sacramento, California	Downtown Street Location
April 10	12	Cedar Rapids, Iowa	Nightclub
May 1	12	Lafayette, Louisiana	Downtown Street Location
May 13	17	Milwaukee, Wisconsin	Public Street following NBA Game
May 14	13	Buffalo New York	Supermarket
May 24	39	Uvalde, Texas	Elementary School
June 4	14	Philadelphia, Pennsylvania	Popular Night Time Town Destination
June 5	14	Chattanooga, Tennessee	Nightclub
July 4	55	Highland Park, Illinois	Public Parade
October 31	14	Chicago, Illinois	Park Event
November 19-20	24	Colorado Springs, Colorado	Gay Nightclub

Table 8.1 *Fifteen Highest Total # Injuries & Deaths from Mass Shootings in the U.S. in 2022*

Source: Estimates from Wikipedia

This chapter's focus is on *actions that bystanders at locations where a mass shooting is taking place* can take to reduce gun deaths and injuries. The following two examples illustrate heroic acts from two of the mass shootings listed in Table 8.1, ones that would have had more victims had they not "stepped up":

At the mass shooting in Colorado Springs in November of 2022 at a gay club, a shooter "opened fire with an AR-15, killing five people and injuring at least 25 in less than a minute, before being tackled by a patron who is being hailed as a hero."[4] The "hero" was a war veteran who "jumped on the 300-pound gunman from behind and pinned him to the ground."[5] In an interview he shared, "I had to do something ... He was not going to kill my family."[6]

In Buffalo, New York, on May 14, 2022, a racially motivated mass shooting occurred at a Tops Friendly supermarket with the gunman killing 10 people, all of whom were black, and injuring another 3. A store employee was "credited with saving lives by hiding customers and colleagues in a freezer."[7] And even though the shooter shot through the coolers, the employee had created a barricade of milk cartons that stopped the bullets from entering. The "hero" was a 29-year-old father of five. In an interview with ABC News, he shared that he felt as if he was "on autopilot, just moving without thinking."[8]

One impactful specific "heroic" behavior is highlighted in this chapter, that of saving lives by **stopping the bleeding of gunshot victims**. As stated by the U.S. Department of Homeland Security, "No matter how fast professional emergency responders arrive, bystanders will always be first on the scene. A person who is bleeding can die from blood loss within five minutes, therefore it is important to quickly stop the blood loss. Those nearest to someone with life threatening injuries are best positioned to provide first care."[9]

A Social Marketing Approach

Purpose & Focus

The STOP THE BLEED® campaign was launched in 2015 with a call to action to begin training more people to become immediate responders.[10] Endorsed by the American College of Surgeons, STB *encourages bystanders to become trained, equipped and empowered to help in a bleeding emergency such as a mass shooting, before professional help arrives*.[11] Partners of STB include organizations such as the U.S. Department of Defense, Homeland Security, FEMA and the American College of Emergency Physicians. As a grassroots movement, it collaborates with a variety of community-based organizations including schools, commercial entities, health care organizations, non-profit organizations, civic organizations, veteran's organizations, and local governmental agencies.[12]

Priority Audiences & Desired Behaviors

STB's intent is to influence *youth and adults* to *take an instructional STB course* to prepare themselves to help injured people following a traumatic event such as a mass shooting. In many respects, it is similar to receiving a training in CPR, the emergency lifesaving procedure performed when the heart stops beating.

A midstream audience the coalition focuses on are *elected officials* at the state and national levels, having trained numerous members of Congress, state officials, and their staff members. The training is intended to garner their support for the program, as well as increase their personal skills in helping to save a life if they are a bystander at a mass shooting.

Audience Insights

STB reports that potential participants in the training course have several concerns and frequently asked questions related to course features:[13]

- How long is the course?
- How hard are the recommended steps to do?
- How much does the STB course cost?
- Where can I find a list and location for an upcoming course?
- How do I set up a course for my school or community?
- Are courses available online?
- If I complete the course successfully, do a I get a completion certificate? How?

Key Strategies

Product: The STB *course* typically lasts no more than 90 minutes, and is developed using science-based guidelines that cover basic components of the "How To" steps including:[14]

- Identify whether bleeding is life-threatening.
- Determine whether a trauma first aid kit is available.
- Properly apply pressure to wounds.
- Properly pack a deep wound with clean cloth or bandages and apply pressure.
- Properly use a tourniquet if available and, if bleeding of a limb doesn't stop, use direct pressure.

The course uses video demonstrations, interactive learnings, and spontaneous quizzes.[15] A formal presentation is followed by hands-on standard practices for applying direct pressure, packing a wound, and using a tourniquet to stop bleeding. A downloadable Save a Life Flowchart provides a *tangible and sustainable instructional summary* of the "how to" steps. The program provides *training kits* to organizations conducting approved training courses, and *bleeding control kits* in public venues such as schools, places of worship and stadiums.[16]

Price: Typically, there is no charge for a course, with almost 80,000 instructors available nationwide volunteering their time and expertise.[17] However, in situations where a course has been formed and offered by some other organization, there may be fees to cover course expenses.[18] A *monetary incentive* strategy includes a potential scholarship for high school students who submit a 1-2 minute video, or write a 250-500 word essay, that addresses specific topics such as how STB helped, or can help, at an accident before emergency responders arrive. Winning students receive a scholarship towards post-secondary education and their schools receive free STOP THE BLEED® kits.[19] A *nonmonetary incentive* is the course completion certificate.

Place: The STB website contains a list of upcoming available courses, including how and where to set up a course for a local group. The "lecture" portion of the course is available online, and can also be found at the STB website. The skills portion of the course is in-person, and is required to complete the course.[20] Those interested in taking a course can also contact their local public health department, hospitals and clinics, emergency medical services, or fire and police department to see if they offer a training.[21]

Promotion: Aside from the organization's website, numerous communications strategies are employed including public relations, ones such as:[22]

- A testimonial from a physician who was interviewed on an "All Things Considered" segment of a public radio station encouraged listeners to visit the STB website and find nearby classes.
- National STOP THE BLEED® Month was established in 2019, declaring the month of May to be one for a recurring annual promotion to encourage the public to take an approved training course.
- Special news coverage highlighted the first STB course in Antarctica, one hosted by the medical team at the Amundsen-Scott South Pole station.

Results

In 2020, a headline on STB's website sharing progress states: "The only thing more tragic than a death from bleeding ... is if that death could have been prevented."[23] Since the STB initiative launched in 2017:[24]

- 2.4 million people have completed the *course training*.
- 117,222 *instructors* have been trained to lead courses.
- 134,510 courses have been offered *in-person*.
- 118 *countries* around the world offer the course.

Progress has also been made in terms of legislative support including the following examples:

- Several states in the U.S. have enacted legislation to support the core strategies of the STB program including:[25]
    o Texas and Indiana passed laws to have STB kits and trainings in schools.

o Georgia included costs to install STB kits in schools a part of the state's budget.

o Illinois's Terrorism Taskforce is installing STB kits in schools.

o Arkansas passed a bill requiring high school students to participate in STB training as a requirement for graduation.

o North Carolina's legislature approved funding for a pilot program to train public school teachers in Transylvania County.

o On September 28, 2022, the California State Legislature and Governor Gavin Newsom enacted Assembly Bill 2260 requiring the installation of trauma bleeding control kits in newly constructed public and private buildings throughout the state.[26]

Applicable Behavior Change Theories

The Theory of Reasoned Action[27] states that the best predictor of a person's behavior is his or her intention to act, and that intention is determined significantly by perceived benefits, potential costs, and beliefs about one's ability to actually perform the behavior (e.g., self-efficacy). Clearly the training course framework for STB is aligned with this theory, emphasizing how critical their intervention would be to save a life; ensuring the training is accessible and free; and providing clear instructions that are singular (e.g., apply pressure) and sequential (e.g., begin by assessing whether the wound is life-threatening and, if so, check to see if a trauma kit is accessible).

The STB program is also aligned with *The Ecological Model*[28] that emphasizes the most powerful behavior change interventions simultaneously influence multiple factors including *individual factors* (e.g., skills), *relationship factors* (e.g., social networks at mass gatherings), *community factors* (e.g., local health care organizations and schools), and *societal factors* (e.g., involvement of Homeland Security and American College of Surgeons in the program).

Social Marketing Principles Contributing to Success[29]

The continued sustainability and impact of the STB program seems likely, and is supported by the integration of several social marketing principles contributing to its success:

- The brief training, the *product,* clearly helps participants successfully prepare for and perform the emergency response.
- Trainings are *brief and accessible,* offered in a variety of venues.
- The potential *benefit* stressed, that of saving a life, is one perceived to be valued and likely to be realized.
- *Monetary costs* are minimal.
- A *nonmonetary incentive,* the completion certificate, is valued.
- *Sponsors and community partners* are ones considered to be credible and trustworthy (e.g., emergency physicians and first responders).

References

¹ CNN, "Mass Shootings in the US Fast Facts" (May 2023), accessed at https://www.cnn.com/2023/01/24/us/mass-shootings-fast-facts/index.html

² GUN VIOLENCE ARCHIVE, "Gun Violence Archive, 2022" (December 2022), accessed at https://www.gunviolencearchive.org/

³ WIKIPEDIA, "List of mass shootings in the United States in 2022" (December 2022), accessed at https://en.wikipedia.org/wiki/List_of_mass_shootings_in_the_United_States_in_2022

⁴ THE WEEK, "Massacre at a gay club in Colorado Springs" (December 2, 2022), p.5.

⁵ Ibid.

⁶ Ibid.

⁷ abcNEWS, "After saving lives in Buffalo mass hooting, store worker opens up about trauma" (November 14, 2022), accessed at https://abcnews.go.com/US/saving-lives-buffalo-mass-shooting-store-worker-opens/story?id=92241881

⁸ Ibid.

⁹ U.S. Homeland Security, "Stop the Bleed" (October 2022), accessed at https://www.dhs.gov/stopthebleed.

¹⁰The White House Archives, "FACTSHEET: Bystander: "Stop the Bleed: (October 2015), accessed at https://obamawhitehouse.archives.gov/the-press-office/2015/10/06/fact-sheet-bystander-stop-bleed-broad-private-sector-support-effort-save

¹¹ U.S. Homeland Security, "Stop the Bleed" (October 2022), accessed at https://www.dhs.gov/stopthebleed

¹² STOP THE BLEED®, "About Us", (2022), accessed at https://stopthebleedcoalition.org/about/

¹³ STOP THE BLEED®, "Learn More", (2022), accessed at https://www.stopthebleed.org/learn-more/

¹⁴ Intermountain® Healthcare, "How Bystanders Can Help Save Lives After a Mass Shooting", (February 2018), accessed at https://intermountainhealthcare.org/blogs/topics/live-well/2018/02/how-bystanders-can-help-save-lives-after-a-mass-shooting/

[15] STOP THE BLEED® , "New Online Course Available" (2022), accessed at https://www.stopthebleed.org/training/

[16] STOP THE BLEED®, "Our Progress" (2020), accessed at https://www.stopthebleed.org/learn-more/progress-goals/

[17] Ibid.

[18] STOP THE BLEED®, "Learn More", (2022), accessed at https://www.stopthebleed.org/learn-more/

[19] STOP THE BLEED®, "Scholarship Program", (2022), accessed https://stopthebleedproject.org/#!/trainathon

[20] STOP THE BLEED®, "Learn More", (2022), accessed at https://www.stopthebleed.org/learn-more/

[21] U.S. Homeland Security, "Stop the Bleed" (October 2022), accessed at https://www.dhs.gov/stopthebleed.

[22] STOP THE BLEED®, "Learn More", (2022), accessed at https://www.stopthebleed.org/learn-more/

[23] STOP THE BLEED®, "Our Progress" (2020), accessed at https://www.stopthebleed.org/learn-more/progress-goals/

[24] Ibid.

[25] STOP THE BLEED®, "STOP THE BLEED Legislative Updates" (2019-2022), accessed at https://www.stopthebleed.org/learn-more/advocate-promote-support/.

[26] American College of Surgeons, "American College of Surgeons applauds passage of STOP THE BLEED® bill in California" (September 28, 2022), accessed at https://www.stopthebleed.org/learn-more/

[27] N. Lee, P. Kotler, and J. Colehour, *Social Marketing: Behavior Change for Good,* 7th Ed. (Thousand Oaks, CA: SAGE, 2024), p.82.

[28] Ibid. p.86.

[29] N. Lee, P. Kotler, and J. Colehour, *Social Marketing: Behavior Change for Good,* 7th Ed. (Thousand Oaks, CA: SAGE, 2024)

Chapter 9

Public Event Attendees Having an Exit Plan

Background

This chapter focuses on influencing protective behaviors among those present at a *mass shooting incident*, ones that can reduce the number of victims and severity of injuries. As noted in earlier chapters, a mass shooting is defined by the FBI as one when there were four or more victims killed, not including the shooter.[1] Two recommended social marketing approaches to reduce potential deaths and injuries during these incidents are highlighted:

- Influencing *individuals* to be prepared to take protective actions when present at a mass shooting
- Influencing *facility managers* to have a response plan in place in the event of a mass shooting

Both approaches are aligned with a principle that preparation is key. "A rapid, safe, and successful response to a mass shooting incident requires preparation...Recent mass shootings have demonstrated the need to prepare local, regional, state and federal resources for these events."[2] For both of the highlighted approaches in this chapter, preparation includes identifying clear actions before the incident occurs, similar to what individuals are "taught" to do when approaching a railroad crossing (e.g., Stop. Look. Listen.), and to what standard evacuation plans recommend in the case of a fire in an office building (e.g., head to the nearest Fire Escape). For both approaches, basic tools and information are recommended to prepare for and respond to a mass shooting, and are outlined in this chapter.

A Social Marketing Approach

Preparedness for Individuals

Purpose, Focus & Priority Audience

A variety of organizations and governmental agencies including the Federal Emergency Management Agency (FEMA), an agency of the Department of Homeland Security, have developed recommended protective actions related to mass shootings for *individuals who frequent large facilities and public events,* ones such as shopping malls, transit stations, sports arenas, theaters, libraries, restaurants, bars, and churches. Actions are intended to *reduce death and injuries at mass shootings* by *improving chances of escape and survival.*

Desired Behavior

One of the most frequently promoted phrases, one supported by FEMA, summarizes recommended actions in the event of a mass shooting, or active shooter in a public location. First, *Know the Exits,* and then *Run. Hide. Fight.*[3] As noted earlier, this could be considered similar to other recommended emergency response actions including *Drop. Cover. Hold.* in the event of an earthquake. As FEMA posts on its website, "Recent national tragedies remind us that the risk is real. Taking a few steps now can help you react quickly when every second counts ... Be prepared for an active shooter, an individual engaged in attempting to kill people in a confined space or populated area."[4]

Audience Insights

For organizations promoting the *Know the Exits* and *Run. Hide. Fight.* actions, several audience insights need to be addressed. Reasons many are not prepared for the first step of *knowing the exits* in the facility include:

- We don't think we are at risk.
- We didn't know it is a good idea to identify the exits when we arrive.
- We forget to check when we get there.

Concerns with additional major steps include:

- We may not *run* right away as we: don't know where to run to; are worried it will make it more likely we will be seen; are not fit enough to run; need to gather our belongings; or don't want to leave others we are with behind.
- We may not *hide* because we want to escape, are concerned we'll be found, or don't see a safe place to go.
- We may not *fight*, primarily because we don't have equipment, don't feel strong enough, or are afraid to get close to the shooter, resulting in getting shot.

Key Strategies

Referred to as a public safety campaign, promotional efforts feature detailed instructions and explanations for each of the major steps, ones made available primarily on line and include:[5]

- **KNOW** *the exits* when you arrive. When you enter a facility, whether a shopping mall or cinema or restaurant, take note of exit signs, ideally locating several since a shooter might enter through one of them. If available, consider choosing seats close to these exits.

- **RUN** *away from the shooter.* Leave things behind and, if safe to do so, warn others nearby.
- **HIDE** *if you can't get away safely.* Ideally, hide in a place where you can lock the doors, bolt the doors, or behind large objects that are sturdy enough to protect from a bullet.
- **QUIET.** FEMA recommends silencing electronic devices and communicating with police silently, such as through text messages, or by putting a sign in an exterior window.
- **FIGHT** *as a last resort to defend yourself.* Search to find objects around you that you can use for defense, such as chairs and fire extinguishers.

Results/Examples of Implementation

The following two examples demonstrate that recommended protective actions are familiar to some:

In July of 2022, CNN interviewed several people regarding mass shootings and how this had affected their lives. One with a father of four shared that he had recently attended a high school graduation with his family and that, as he sat down in the auditorium, "he felt vulnerable, and he couldn't help but mentally plan his family's escape if gunfire erupted, identifying exits and potential hiding places ... It's one of the first things that now crosses my mind. What would we do? Where would we go? How would we hide?" [6]

In October of 2017, a segment featured on KHQ television news featured an interview with a police department Lieutenant regarding the recent mass shooting at a Las Vegas strip. He commented that "We don't have to physically experience shootings to have a plan. Start thinking about it now and be prepared and have that plan in your brain ... Just remember the words, *run, hide, fight.*" He went on to emphasize the importance of knowing the emergency exits, and if not able to escape "get behind something that can stop or slow a bullet."[7]

Preparedness for Facility Managers

Purpose & Focus

This second featured social marketing approach has a similar purpose *to reduce deaths and injuries from mass shootings,* but in this case with a focus on *emergency action plans,* ones similar to those developed in the case of crisis such as a hazardous fire in a building which include fire drills, sprinkler systems, building codes and more.

Priority Audiences & Desired Behaviors

As described by a publication of the L. Douglas Wilder School of Government and Public Affairs, "Emergency action plans enable stakeholder organizations, property managers, emergency responders and local law enforcement to collaborate on effective steps to take in an active shooter situation."[8] Organizations are encouraged to *develop an Active Shooter Emergency Action Plan using a template developed by Homeland Security,* and to then practice the plan regularly to ensure others based in the facility know what to do, and where to go in the event of a shooting.

Audience Insights

Barriers likely needed to be addressed include perceptions of low risk, amount of time needed to access the template and complete the plan, current presence of security guards, need for multiagency/ organization coordination, and potential financial concerns for cost of any recommended equipment or structural changes. Benefits to highlight would certainly be the opportunity to save the lives of staff, customers, and visitors.

Key Strategies.

Homeland Security provides access to several resources for completing the recommended *Active Shooter Emergency Action Plan*, including a downloadable template and instructional videos. The template includes six planning steps: [9]

1. **Form a Collaborative Planning Team** with at least four to ten members, one representing a cross-section of employees including ones from key segments such as human resources, security managers, facility managers, information technology managers, legal advisors, and communication managers.

2A. **Develop an Active Shooter Prevention Plan**, one encompassing three areas: 1) a training for employees to recognize behaviors on a Pathway to Violence; 2) a system for reporting tailored to your organization; and 3) a description of the organization's intervention process.

2B. **Conduct a Risk Assessment**, that identifies threats, vulnerabilities, and consequences for the organization in the case of a mass shooting/active shooter incident.

3. **Establish Goals and Objectives,** with goals being broad statements of what personnel, equipment and resources are intended to achieve, and objectives specifying actions that participants in the process are to accomplish.

4. **Access Courses of Action,** to accomplish specific goals and objectives.

5. **Draft Plan and Approve**, one that includes all essential information and instructions that protect against an active shooter.

6. **Train Personnel and Conduct Exercises,** including at new employee orientations, staff meetings and via internal communications.

Instructive videos guide organizations in completing the six planning steps, such as reviewing the choices for evacuation, hiding, or, as an option of last resort, confronting the shooter. They also include subject matter experts who share their unique insights, ones including perspectives of active shooter survivors and first responders.[10]

Results/Examples

One example of a state's acceptance and recommendation for this planning tool is a statement from the Tennessee Emergency Management Agency that the planning guide, plan template, and video will "enhance preparedness through a 'whole community' approach by providing products, tools, and resources to help you prepare for and respond to an active shooter incident."[11]

A website of the Office of Safety Management describes the value of the Active Shooter Preparedness Plan, commenting that "Active shooter situations can be random, with rapid and unpredictable events unfolding. Thinking about and practicing the proper response now can boost your chance of survival through the event, and the aftermath."[12]

Applicable Behavior Change Theories

The *Health Belief Model*[13] addresses one of the major barriers to this desired action of creating an emergency plan and, in the event of a shooting, engaging in specific desired actions. As noted, a major consideration, deterrent, for both audiences was *perceived susceptibility*, the likelihood that there would be a mass shooting at an event or location where they would be in attendance. Strategies in this program addressed this by highlighting, front and center, the potential *perceived benefits of taking the recommended action*, that of escaping death or injury from a shooting.

The *Stages of Change Theory*[14] suggests that the clear attractive audience for developing an escape plan in the event of a mass shooting, for both the individual as well as facility manager segments, are those in the *Contemplation* stage, those who acknowledge there is a potential risk and are beginning to think seriously about it. Campaign strategies were developed to then move them to *Preparation*, with facility managers supported with tools to develop emergency plans, and individuals supported to "easily remember" what to do in the event of a shooting incident, "Run. Hide. Fight".

Social Marketing Principles Contributing to Success[15]

- A principle applicable to both segments is that of that of *taking advantage of prior and existing successful campaigns*. For individuals, the memorable and instructive slogan of "Run. Hide. Fight." was inspired, perhaps, by the similar well known injury prevention campaigns "Drop. Cover. Hold", and "Stop. Look. Listen." For facility managers, having a plan in place for emergency shootings would be similar to having plans in the event of fires and earthquakes.
- The campaign programs also focused on *single, doable behaviors,* ones that were promoted as having *significant potential impact*.

References

[1] ABC News, "The 11 mass deadly school shootings that happened since Columbine" (April 19, 2019), accessed at https://abcnews.go.com/US/11-mass-deadly-school-shootings-happened-columbine/story?id=62494128

[2] Government Technology, "Planning, Preparation Needed to Respond to Mass Shootings" (July 2009), accessed at https://www.govtech.com/em/disaster/planning-preparation-needed-to.html.

[3] FEMA, "Active Shooter" (n.d.), accessed at https://community.fema.gov/ProtectiveActions/s/article/Active-Shooter

[4] Ibid.

[5] FEMA, "Be Prepared for an Active Shooter" (March 2018), accessed at BE PREPARED FOR AN ACTIVE SHOOTER (ready.gov)

[6] CNN, "America's struggle with mass shootings has changed how these people live their lives" (July 5, 2022), accessed at https://www.cnn.com/2022/06/26/us/gun-violence-america-fear/index.html

[7] KHQ, "How to improve your chances of escaping a mass shooting" (October 2, 2017) accessed at https://www.khq.com/news/how-to-improve-your-chances-of-escaping-a-mass-shooting/article_fc3af011-573c-5de8-becb-429257e18441.html

[8] Virginia Commonwealth University, L. Douglas Wilder School of Government and Public Affairs, "The Role of Emergency Preparedness in Preventing Mass Shootings" (November 2022), accessed at https://online wilder.vcu.edu/blog/preventing-mass-shootings/ .

[9] U.S. Department of Homeland Security, "Emergency Action Plan Guide" (n.d.), accessed at https://www.cisa.gov/sites/default/files/publications/active-shooter-emergency-action-plan-112017-508v2.pdf

[10] TN Department of Military, "Active Shooter Preparedness" (n.d.), accessed at https://www.tn.gov/tema/prepare/active-shooter-preparedness.html

[11] Ibid.

[12] OSM, "Active Shooter Preparedness" (n.d.), accessed at https://www.safety manualosha.com/active-shooter-preparednes/

[13] N. Lee, P. Kotler, and J. Colehour *Social Marketing: Behavior Change for Good,* 7th Ed. (Thousand Oaks, CA: SAGE, 2024), pp.80-81.

[14] Ibid., pp.78-79.

[15] N. Lee, P. Kotler, and J. Colehour *Social Marketing: Behavior Change for Good,* 7th Ed. (Thousand Oaks, CA: SAGE, 2024)

Chapter 10

Communities
Reducing Youth Handgun Carrying

Background

CDC's Healthy People initiative sets data-driven national objectives to improve health and well-being over the decade. Relative to reducing *gun carrying among adolescents*, the stated objective is to **move from 4.4% in 2019 to 3.7%, a 16% decrease, by 2030.**[1]

In 2023, an article published by the *Journal of the American Medical Association (JAMA) Network Open* featured a research study titled: "Effect of the Communities That Care Prevention System on Adolescent Handgun Carrying."[2] Several highlighted statistics inspired the research study, as well as the need for this chapter's topic on youth homicides:[3]

- Firearm injury is the leading cause of death among children and adolescents in the U.S.
- 64% of these firearm deaths were homicide.
- Every day, approximately 7 young people were victims of homicide.
- Prevalence of gun carrying among adolescents is greater in nonmetropolitan areas.

Federal data reports provide additional insights related to profiles of youth gun death victims, noting that gun death rates are as much as *6 times higher among males than females*, and that there is a *disproportionate burden on ethnic and racial minority youth* citing that gun homicide is the:[4]

- Leading cause of death for African American youth
- Second leading cause of death for Hispanic youth
- Third leading cause for American Indian/Alaska Native Youth
- Fourth leading cause among White and Asian/Pacific Islander Youth

Additional related study findings provide a rationale for this chapter's focus on gun carrying among youth:

> "Data from the National Longitudinal Study of Adolescent to Adult Health were used to assess the long-term associations between gun ownership and gun carrying in late adolescence and violence and violent victimization in early adulthood. Results from propensity score matching analyses suggest **gun carrying, but not gun ownership, is associated with a higher risk of experiencing violent victimization and engaging in violence with a weapon**. Efforts to curb firearm-related violence should consider focusing on those who carry guns for additional counseling about these risks."[5]

Multiple approaches are valid and important to preventing gun carrying among youth including the following noted by a study published by The National Academy of Medicine:[6]

- Prevent youth access to firearms in the home.
- Prevent diversion of guns to youth, including those from the underground gun market.
- Reduce illegal carrying through increased police enforcement.
- Identify hot spots for interventions, and offer services to facilitate legal and safe lifestyles.

Given this book highlights social marketing approaches to inspire behavior change, examples presented in this chapter are most aligned with the fourth approach noted above, that of offering services to facilitate change.

A Social Marketing Approach

Purpose & Focus

This chapter features efforts to *reduce youth gun homicides* with a focus on *youth handgun carrying,* one noted earlier as having a strong corollary to actual homicides. Examples of alternative/additional areas of focus for reducing youth gun homicides include family members and friends safely securing their guns, an approach highlighted in Chapter 3 to reduce youth suicides, underscoring the positive impact that safe gun storage can have on this social issue.

Priority Audiences & Desired Behaviors

In July of 2022, CDC published findings from their Youth Risk Behavior Survey of 2019 that gun carrying among high school students in the previous 12 months was at 6.8% for males and 1.9% for females.[7] It was noted that this did not include carrying a gun for hunting or sports.

These findings, as well as those previously cited, suggest that a priority segment to influence for efforts to reduce handgun carrying are **male high school youth who have carried a gun at least once in the previous 12 months, especially those who "had experienced violence, suicidal ideation or attempts, or substance use."[8]**

Audience Insights

An article published by the National Academy of Medicine included findings from an extensive study of youth involved in guns and violence. Regarding why youth were carrying guns, the most reported *desired benefit was self-protection.*[9] Factors noted as *determinants of adolescent gun carrying* include the following:

- **Gun Availability**: For firearms used outside the home, almost a half (47%) were acquired from "the street or black market", and more than a third (36%) were acquired from a friend or family member.[10]
- **Delinquent/Criminal Behaviors:** Juvenile gun carrying is associated with several behaviors including alcohol and substance abuse, fighting, gang membership and drug selling.[11]
- **Social Networks:** Those tied to social networks of criminal offenders are at greatest risk of carrying guns, "letting it be known that they were armed and willing to kill so as to deter others who might consider challenging, robbing, or disrespecting them."[12] Further, it was noted they were not motivated by a need to "gain social recognition or status among their peers."[13]
- **Fear-Driven Protection:** This factor is especially relevant for those that "live in neighborhoods that put them at high risk for being shot and therefore feel the need to be armed with a gun."[14] In addition, fear of risk is also greater among those experiencing victimization in the past, having a family member who had been shot, or being a witness of violence.[15]

Key Strategies

An example of a program that includes a social marketing, behavior change, approach to reduce youth gun carrying is the **Communities**

that Care (CTC) prevention system.[16] As stated by Dr. Ali Rowhani Rahbar at the University of Washington, this "community-based prevention program could help reduce the number of kids who die from gun violence. Their work can be implemented by community members – not lawmakers."[17]

Developed at University of Washington Social Development Research Group (SDRG) and implemented with support from the Center for Communities That Care, which is housed within SDRG, "CTC is an evidence-based prevention system that assists communities in using science-based solutions to foster the healthy development of young people. The Center for CTC is currently helping to implement the system in 150 communities nationwide, in addition to 14 countries."[18] Using a structured five-phase planning process tailored to local strengths and needs, CTC is designed to help coalitions use local risk and protective factor data collected from young people in the community to establish prevention priorities. Coalitions are then supported in selecting evidence-based strategies in order to achieve better health outcomes for young people community wide. Program strategies include a variety of custom-designed offerings including parent training, school-based programs (e.g., drug prevention curricula), and after-school programs (e.g., mentoring).[19] Inspiring outcomes for one program are shared in this next example.

Example

"Effect of the Communities That Care Prevention System on Adolescent Handgun Carrying"[20]

The study in the *JAMA Network Open* article noted earlier was led by University of Washington researchers, funded by CDC, and supported by others including the National Institutes of Health. The **objective** of the study was to confirm, or not, that the Communities

That Care (CTC) model could be effective in reducing the prevalence of adolescent handgun carrying, with a focus on those growing up in rural areas in the United States. At the time the research was undertaken in 2003, prior studies had demonstrated the impact of CTC on reducing several youth risk behaviors (e.g., drug use), but there had not been ones focusing on its potential impact on reducing handgun carrying.[21]

Research Methods

Researchers conducted a community-randomized trial within 24 small towns in 7 states, with participants assigned randomly either to programs that would implement the CTC approach, or to a control group. Participants in the intervention, as well as control groups, were youths attending public schools in grade 5 who received permission from their parents to participate in the research. Students were repeatedly surveyed through grade 12, with a 92% participant retention rate. Outcomes were assessed from 2003 to 2011, and analyses were conducted in 2022.[22]

At the core of the survey of these youth from grades 6 through grades 12 was the following question:

"How many times in the past year (12 months) have you carried a handgun?" Response options included: never, 1 to 2 times, 3 to 5 times, 6 to 9 times, 10 to 19 times, 20 to 29 time, 30 to 39 times, or 40 or more times.[23]

Interventions

Community coalitions began implementation of between 1 and 5 CTC prevention programs starting with the 2004 to 2005 school year, and then annually thereafter, with researchers reporting that 18 different school, family, and community-based programs were implemented across the 12 intervention communities.[24] Details on interventions described in the article included:

"CTC communities each identified locally specific related risk factors and low protective factors for adolescent problem behaviors in individual, peer, family, school, and community domains according to survey data from students in grade 6, 8, 10 and 12 in those communities. They were asked to focus their prevention plans on programs for youths ages 10 to 14 years and their families and schools so that possible effects on drug use and delinquency could be observed within the initial 5-year study period."[25]

"A coalition of community stakeholders received training and technical assistance to install CTC, used local epidemiologic data to identify elevated risk factors and low protective factors for adolescent behavioral problems, and implemented tested preventive interventions for youth, their families, and schools."[26] Program strategies implemented "included parent training programs (e.g., group-based and self-administered programs), after-school programs (e.g., skills-based interventions, mentoring, and tutoring services), and school-based programs (e.g., drug prevention curricula and schoolwide organizational change strategies)."[27]

Results

"Youths in CTC communities were significantly less likely to report handgun carrying at a given grade than those in control communities. The most pronounced effects were observed in grade 7, grade 8, and grade 9 ... Overall, **CTC reduced the prevalence of past-year handgun carrying by 27% at a given grade and by 24% cumulatively through grade 12.**"[28]

References

[1] CDC, "Reduce gun carrying among adolescents" (n.d.), accessed at Reduce gun carrying among adolescents — IVP-12 - Healthy People 2030 | health.gov

[2] A., Rowhani-Rahbar et al., *JAMA Network Open*, "Effect of the Communities That Care Prevention System on Adolescent Handgun Carrying"(2023), accessed at DOI: 10.1001/jamanetworkopen.2023.6699

[3] Goldstick, JE, Cunningham , Carter PM, "Current cause of death in children and adolescents in the United States" N Engl J Med 2022; 386:1955-1956 DOI: 10.1056/NEJMc2201761

[4] Youth.Gov, "Federal Data" (n.d.), accessed at https://youth.gov/youth-topics/violence-prevention/federal-data

[5] J. Kelsay, et al., National Library of Medicine, "The Association Between Adolescent Gun Ownership and Gun Carrying and Adulthood Violence and Victimization" (Feb. 2021), accessed at https://pubmed.ncbi.nlm.nih.gov/33443229/

[6] D. Webster, et al., Institute of Medicine, National Academy of Medicine, "Youth Acquisition and Carrying of Firearms in the U.S." (2014), accessed at https://nap.nationalacademies.org/resource/21814/Youth-Acquisition-Carrying-Firearms-US.pdf

[7] CDC MMWR, "Gun Carrying Among Youths, by Demographic Characteristics, Associated Violence Experiences, and Risk Behaviors – United States, 2017-2019" T. Simon et al., (July 2022), accessed at https://www.cdc.gov/mmwr/volumes/71/wr/pdfs/mm7130a1-H.pdf

[8] Ibid.

[9] D. Webster, et al., Institute of Medicine, National Academy of Medicine, "Youth Acquisition and Carrying of Firearms in the U.S." (2014), p.18, accessed at https://nap.nationalacademies.org/resource/21814/Youth-Acquisition-Carrying-Firearms-US.pdf

[10] Ibid. p.5.

[11] Ibid. p.17.

[12] Ibid. p.18.

[13] Ibid. p.18.

[14] Ibid. p.19.

[15] Ibid. p.19.

[16] The Center for Communities That Care (2023), accessed at https://www.communitiesthatcare.net/

[17] abcNEWS, "University of Washington researchers say their prevention program could reduce gun violence deaths in children" (April 2023), M. Ruprecht et al., accessed at https://abcnews.go.com/US/university-washington-researchers-prevention-program-reduce-gun-violence/story?id=98482269

[18] UW News, "Community-based prevention system linked to reduced handgun carrying among youth growing up in rural areas" (April 2023), A. Woods, accessed at https://www.washington.edu/news/2023/04/06/community-based-prevention-system-linked-to-reduced-handgun-carrying-among-youth-growing-up-in-rural-areas/

[19] abcNEWS, "University of Washington researchers say their prevention program could reduce gun violence deaths in children" (April 2023), M. Ruprecht et al., accessed at https://abcnews.go.com/US/university-washington-researchers-prevention-program-reduce-gun-violence/story?id=98482269

[20] JAMA Network Open, "Effect of the Communities That Care Prevention System on Adolescent Handgun Carrying"(April 2023), A. Rowhani-Rahbar et. al, accessed at https://jamanetwork.com/journals/jamanetworkopen/fullarticle/2803249

[21] Ibid.

[22] Ibid., p.1.

[23] Ibid., p.5.

[24] Ibid., p.3.

[25] Ibid., p.3.

[26] Ibid., p.1.

[27] Ibid., p.4.

[28] Ibid., p.1.

Chapter 11

Gang Members
Participating in Group Meetings

Background

The FBI reports on one of their websites in 2023 that there are an estimated 33,000 criminally active violent gangs in the U.S., with three major categories being street gangs, motorcycle gangs and prison gangs.[1] Many are organized with activities to control neighborhoods, and others to boost their illegal money-making activities, ones which include robbery, drug and gun trafficking, human trafficking, and fraud.[2]

Gang violence statistics in the U.S. for 2022 indicate the following levels of concern and concentration, ones that inspired having a chapter in this book to address reducing gang gun violence:

- Although gang members constitute less than .5% of a city's population, they contribute to as much as 70% of homicide and gun violence.[3]
- 13% of all murders are associated with gangs.[4]
- 2,000 murders every year are gang related homicides.[5]
- 49% of violent crime is gang related.[6]
- 67% of gang related killings were in cities with more than 100,000 citizens.[7]

What is known about the profile of gang members? The U.S. Department of Justice reports that: "Most participants in gang crimes tend to be young, male, and either Black of Hispanic ... The average age of the arrested gang offender is seventeen or eighteen years."[8] It is noted, in addition, that many gang members are ones who continue to commit crimes even after serving time in jail.[9]

Given the significant impact of gang-related crimes, what major initiatives at the federal level are used to reduce these incidents? Two major anti-gang resources noted by the FBI include:[10]

- The National Gang Intelligence Center integrates gang intelligence from across federal, state, and local law enforcement, and supports law enforcement by sharing timely and accurate information based on this intelligence analysis.
- The Violent Gang Safe Streets Task Force supports federal, state, and local law enforcement agencies to collaboratively pursue violent gangs through sustained, proactive, and coordinated investigations to obtain prosecutions for violence.

This chapter highlights one program strategy supported to reduce gang-related gun violence that has been implemented in several cities across the U.S., one with a strong social marketing approach.

A Social Marketing Approach

Purpose & Focus

The *Group Violence Intervention (GVI)* program, also known by other names including *Operation Ceasefire*, certainly has a similar purpose to most programs, that of intending to *reduce gang-related gun violence*, but, in this case, one with a unique focus. Many gun violence reduction programs focus on law enforcement tactics.[11] Alternatively, GVI programs focus on *a community partnership* of law enforcement, community members, and social service agency providers that together develop a strategy to engage with gang members and influence voluntary compliance with laws, deterrence from violent acts, and accessing support services. The partnership may also include members of community faith-based organizations as well as local businesses. The intent is to build the community's capacity "to prevent violence, use enforcement narrowly and strategically, help the most vulnerable people, and improve the legitimacy of police in the eyes of the community."[12]

GVI strategies begin with organizing a *working group* to design and implement a local strategy. The group accesses and analyzes existing data and then collects relevant missing data on gang violence in their community. Of specific interest are patterns of gang violence, locations of violent incidents, and demographic information on those in the community involved specifically in gun violence.[13] This information then informs a targeted outreach and local intervention strategy.

Priority Audiences & Desired Behaviors

Included in the working group's data analysis is an examination of frontline knowledge and real-time data to inform selection of *gangs and gang members in the community who are at highest risk for future gun violence offense*. Factors that create a high priority for outreach include those in geographic areas with a higher than average number of prior incidents and arrests. As noted earlier, the highest risk gang members are most often male youth who are Black or Hispanic.[14] Additionally, they tend to be disproportionately from single-parent households and from families living below the poverty level.[15] It is noted, however, that these gangs do have representation from other age and ethnic groups. Additional informative data as of 2020 includes:

- The average amount of time youth are members of a gang is one to two years, with a common misconception that these members have a tough time leaving.[16]
- 8% of youth join a gang by their twenties.[17]
- 71% of gang members actively use social media, with a significant portion (20%) stating they operate a website or social media page. [18]

What working group members want gang members "to do" is *accept their invitation to in person engagements and, subsequently, receive support services.*

Audience Insights

Barriers

Offers to gang members to engage with community members including law enforcement may be deterred by a lack of trust that they won't be punished for prior incidents. They may also be concerned that by "cooperating" with law enforcement they might experience retaliation from other members of the gang.

Additionally, there are several valued benefits of "the way things are" that might be perceived as in jeopardy including having a sense of support and belonging from fellow gang members, maintaining control of a specific territory/neighborhood, demonstrating power to rivals, and exercising revenge. [19]

Desired Benefits

Perhaps what would be perceived as a benefit of engagement that would outweigh costs is an imagined future where gangs would not be broken apart, but would instead engage in activities that were nonviolent and did not result in criminal offences or harm to others.

Motivators

Features of GVI programs that motivate engagement include the practice that gang members attend gatherings along with other gang members, are ensured they will be respected, and that this will support them to be "alive, safe, and stay out of prison."[20] In addition, they would have ease of access to basic support services, and as efforts increase within communities, a perceived norm for cooperation and receiving support services is likely to be established.

Key Strategy: "Call-Ins"

Once GVI working groups have identified priority gangs and gang members for engagement, members reach out through face to face introductions and/or other options based on available contact information on record, often from prior gang related incidents. Group members might also connect with people close to these members and reach out to them to help with connecting. In some instances, a gang member may be required to respond given terms of their probation or parole.[21]

A first step is the invitation to what is referred to as a "Call-In", or forum, typically a face-to-face meeting between selected gang members and working group members representing each of the community groups. Groups are often held at a community facility, and may last about one hour.[22]

Messages are intended to create strong community norms against violence, ensure gang members understand the legal risks they face, are delivered with respect, and support a new and strong relationship between law enforcement and communities.[23] The U.S. Department of Justice encourages a "two-part" message to be delivered at gatherings: "(a) gun violence must stop immediately or criminal justice agencies will intervene quickly and forcefully against those responsible; and (b) the group is there to support the gang members and youth with intensive services and employment."[24] The City of Philadelphia's GVI program sees the following specific GROUPS message as key:[25]

- "Groups Are Driving Gun Violence."
- "Receive Consequences If You Shoot Or Help If You Want It."
- "Our Community (Including You) Is Hurt By Gun Violence."
- "U Are Connected To Group Violence!"
- "Put Down the Guns."
- "Share This Message With Your Group."

Messengers at the gathering, in addition to members of the working group, often include surviving family members of homicide victims, as well as former gang members:

Workgroup messengers highlight their intention to depart from harmful practices, and instead show respect and support for those with criminal backgrounds, engage openly and honestly about how they work and promote voluntary compliance with the law.[26]

Surviving family members of homicide victims often describe the pain of losing their loved one. The City of Philadelphia, for example, reports that dozens of survivors, most of whom are mothers of murder victims, participate in programs on a voluntary basis almost every weekend for a year.[27]

Former gang members might share their trusted experiences and achievement of desired outcomes, even the possibility of transformation.

Support Services

Given the situation that many participants are currently experiencing high rates of violent victimization, GVI meetings usually wrap up with genuine, unconditional offers for immediate support from a variety of community social service agencies. Representatives of organizations in attendance connect with attendees offering access to basic needs including temporary housing, groceries, mental health counseling, substance abuse support, as well as employment opportunities, skill trainings, educational programs, and transportation assistance. This support is said to give gang members a "path away from risky behavior and toward new and positive relationships. It also demonstrates, beyond the immediate goals of preventing violence, a commitment to the lives of group members."[28] As the GVI program of the City of Philadelphia describes it, "The offer of help is not an alternative to consequences but instead a recognition that some group members may need help changing their behavior."[29]

At conclusion of the gathering, the intention is that gang members and leaders take what they have heard back to their groups, share their trust in community members, including law enforcement, and that desirable services are available for support.

Examples & Results

A USAID study in 2016, reviewed over 30 violence reduction strategies and concluded that GVI "has the largest direct impact on crime and violence, by far, of any intervention."[30]

Promising results from programs, some mentioned in this chapter, include the following:

Philadelphia

In August of 2020, the City of Philadelphia launched a modified version of their GVI strategy, given the need to avoid large group gatherings during COVID 19. Alternatively, they engaged three full time case workers and one supervisor who worked with GVI partners through direct engagement in the community. They became known as Mobile Call-In Teams, with gatherings held via mobile devices and consisting of the same messengers and messages as there were for in person gatherings. In terms of results, in the first 15 months of the initiative the City reported that as of December 2021, Mobile Call-In Teams had conducted approximately 1,191 home visits, and that this resulted in *direct engagements with 302 individual members*. In addition, 239 collateral contacts were made with family members or other influencers of GVI Candidates.[31] A report also shared a quote from a participant:

> "I never had interactions with police like I had during the (engagement). They were serious about stopping gun violence, but they were also really concerned for my (safety). It was a weird encounter. Weird because it was positive not negative ... You can't come to the community with a lock-you-up mentality...but when you come with respect and a sense of care for the people, we will be more open to having a conversation."[32] GVI Participant

Chicago

A U.S. Department of Justice report contained a review of a gun Violence Reduction Strategy (VRS) in Chicago. "The findings indicate that those gang factions who attended a VRS call-in experienced *a 23-percent reduction in overall shooting behavior and a 32-percent reduction in gunshot victimization in the year after treatment compared with similar factions* ... The results of this study suggest that focused intervention efforts such as VRS can produce significant reductions in gun violence, especially gunshot victimization among gangs. Focused programs such as these offer an important alternative to broad, sweeping practices or policies that might otherwise expand the use of the criminal justice system. (publisher abstract modified)."[33]

Boston

A GVI program in Boston, originally known as Operation Ceasefire, reported "the program was responsible for a *63 percent reduction in youth homicide victimization* ... The typical impact is a 35 to 60 percent reduction in community-wide levels of homicides and a significant but sometimes lesser reduction in nonfatal shootings citywide."[34]

Applicable Behavior Change Theories

Creating a community norm[35] is certainly a top of mind theoretical application for this program. Several features of the program build and support this persuasive perception including the gathering in groups for gang members (e.g., others like myself), and involvement of a wide range of community partners.

The Social Cognitive Theory[36] is applicable given that likelihood of attending the group gatherings is influenced by perceptions *that benefits will outweigh costs*, in this case, that community acceptance of their gang and access to social services "will be much better than going to jail." *Perceptions of self-efficacy* is strengthened by knowing gang members will support each other in voluntary compliance.

Social Marketing Principles Contributing To Success[37]

Major principles for success in social marketing efforts are apparent in this case, with the following two especially applicable:

- *Select a Clear Priority Audience*: The process used to identify and prioritize gangs seems central to success in this case. As noted earlier, recognizing that gangs contribute as much as 70 percent of homicides in a city, but constitute only .5% of its population[38], and that gangs are in concentrated geographic locations within the city, supported working group members in their outreach activities, as well as concentration of resources with the most violent of gang members.

- *Use Influential Messengers:* These GVI programs were certainly committed to having key messengers be those that gang members would "believe", especially at the group gatherings. Hearing troublesome stories from *prior gang members* who had not voluntarily abstained from violent crimes was certainly motivating. And even more persuasive was hearing from *those who had followed the voluntary guidelines*, received support services, and ultimately experienced "transformation."

References

[1] FBI, "Gangs" (n.d.), p.1, accessed at https://www.fbi.gov/investigate/violent-crime/gangs.

[2] Ibid.

[3] National Network For Safe Communities at JOHN JAY COLLEGE, "GROUP VIOLENCE INTERVENTION" (n.d.), p.2, accessed at https://nnscommunities.org/wp-content/uploads/2020/08/GVI-Issue-Brief-1.pdf.

[4] Safeatlast, "25 Dreadful Gang Violence Statistics for 2022" (April 2022), p.1, accessed at https://safeatlast.co/blog/gang-violence-statistics/.

[5] Ibid.

[6] Ibid., p.2

[7] Ibid., p.7.

[8] U.S. Department of Justice, "Gang Statistics" (Jan. 2020), accessed at https://www.justice.gov/archives/jm/criminal-resource-manual-103-gang-statistics

[9] FBI, "Gangs" (n.d.), p.1, accessed at https://www.fbi.gov/investigate/violent-crime/gangs.

[10] Ibid.

[11] National Network For Safe Communities at JOHN JAY COLLEGE, "GROUP VIOLENCE INTERVENTION" (n.d.), p.3, accessed at https://nnscommunities.org/wp-content/uploads/2020/08/GVI-Issue-Brief-1.pdf.

[12] Ibid., p.2.

[13] United States Attorney's Office, "Operation Ceasefire and the Safe Community Partnership" (May 2021), accessed at https://www.justice.gov/usao-ndca/operation-ceasefire-and-safe-community-partnership.

[14] Hollie, B., National Council on Family Relations, "Preventing Gun and Gang Violence in the Black Community: A Family Systems Perspective" (January 2019), accessed at Preventing Gun and Gang Violence in the Black Community: A Family Systems Perspective | National Council on Family Relations (ncfr.org)

[15] Hollie, B., National Council on Family Relations, "Preventing Gun and Gang Violence in the Black Community: A Family Systems Perspective" (January 2019), accessed at Preventing Gun and Gang Violence in the Black Community: A Family Systems Perspective | National Council on Family Relations (ncfr.org)

16 Safeatlast, "25 Dreadful Gang Violence Statistics for 2022" (April 2022), accessed at https://safeatlast.co/blog/gang-violence-statistics/.

17 Ibid.

18 Ibid.

19 Ibid.

20 National Network For Safe Communities at JOHN JAY COLLEGE, "GROUP VIOLENCE INTERVENTION" (n.d.), p.2, accessed at https://nnscommunities.org/wp-content/uploads/2020/08/GVI-Issue-Brief-1.pdf

21 Ibid., p.5.

22 City of Philadelphia, "Group Violence Intervention in Philadelphia" (December 2021), p.10, accessed at Jan32022GunViolence-003.pdf (phila.gov).

23 National Network For Safe Communities at JOHN JAY COLLEGE, "GROUP VIOLENCE INTERVENTION" (n.d.), p.5, accessed at https://nnscommunities.org/wp-content/uploads/2020/08/GVI-Issue-Brief-1.pdf

24 U.S. Department of Justice, "Operation Ceasefire and the Safe Community Partnership" (May 2021), p.2., accessed at https://www.justice.gov/usao-ndca/operation-ceasefire-and-safe-community-partnership.

25 City of Philadelphia, "Group Violence Intervention in Philadelphia" (December 2021), p.2, accessed at Jan32022GunViolence-003.pdf (phila.gov).

26 National Network For Safe Communities at JOHN JAY COLLEGE, "GROUP VIOLENCE INTERVENTION" (n.d.), p.5, accessed at https://nnscommunities.org/wp-content/uploads/2020/08/GVI-Issue-Brief-1.pdf.

27 City of Philadelphia, "Group Violence Intervention in Philadelphia" (December 2021), p.7, accessed at Jan32022GunViolence-003.pdf (phila.gov).

28 National Network For Safe Communities at JOHN JAY COLLEGE, "GROUP VIOLENCE INTERVENTION" (n.d.), p.5, accessed at https://nnscommunities.org/wp-content/uploads/2020/08/GVI-Issue-Brief-1.pdf.

29 City of Philadelphia, "Group Violence Intervention in Philadelphia" (December 2021) p.3, accessed at Jan32022GunViolence-003.pdf (phila.gov).

30 National Network For Safe Communities at JOHN JAY COLLEGE, "GROUP VIOLENCE INTERVENTION" (n.d.), p.6, accessed at https://nnscommunities.org/wp-content/uploads/2020/08/GVI-Issue-Brief-1.pdf

31 City of Philadelphia, "Group Violence Intervention in Philadelphia" (December 2021), p.4, accessed at Jan32022GunViolence-003.pdf (phila.gov).

32 Ibid., p.5.

33 U.S. Department of Justice, "Changing the Street Dynamic: Evaluating Chicago's Group Violence Reduction Strategy" (2015), p.1, accessed at https://www.ojp.gov/ncjrs/virtual-library/abstracts/changing-street-dynamic-evaluating-chicagos-group-violence.

[34] National Gang Center, "Group Violence Intervention" (April 2021), accessed at https://nationalgangcenter.ojp.gov/spt/Programs/42.

[35] N. Lee, P. Kotler, and J. Colehour, *Social Marketing: Behavior Change for Good,* 7th Ed. (Thousand Oaks, CA: SAGE, 2024), pp.84-86.

[36] Ibid., p.83.

[37] N. Lee, P. Kotler, and J. Colehour, *Social Marketing: Behavior Change for Good,* 7th Ed. (Thousand Oaks, CA: SAGE, 2024)

[38] National Network For Safe Communities at JOHN JAY COLLEGE, "GROUP VIOLENCE INTERVENTION" (n.d.), p.3., accessed at https://nnscommunities.org/wp-content/uploads/2020/08/GVI-Issue-Brief-1.pdf.

Chapter 12

Neighbors
Greening Abandoned Vacant Lots

Background

This chapter elaborates on a *physical environmental design approach* to reducing gun injuries and deaths. Several research studies and programs are highlighted, documenting that unmaintained abandoned and vacant neighborhood lots, often overgrown with high grasses and dense brush, can provide hiding spots for criminals and their guns. The good news reported in an article published by the *American Journal of Community Psychology* is that "community-engaged greening of vacant lots is associated with **nearly a 40% reduction in assaults and total violent crime** compared to vacant lots not maintained by these groups."[1]

Vacant lots referred to in these studies are parcels of property primarily in residential neighborhoods that are:[2]

- Unoccupied
- Often abandoned and unclaimed
- Not regularly maintained
- Often used for illegal dumping
- Likely to be interspersed throughout a neighborhood
- Frequently located in minority and socially disadvantaged communities

In many cases, houses were once on these lots, fell into disrepair or were demolished. In addition to the CDC's concern for public health and violence related to vacant lots such as these,[3] the Environmental Protection Agency (EPA) also expresses significant community concerns, stating that "these vacant lots are not just unsightly blights on the urban landscape, and breeding grounds for rats, they are a wasted resource. They disrupt a neighborhood's sense of community and lower property values ... The main goal of vacant lot projects and policies is to reclaim these lots and move them into productive use."[4]

The term *"Greening Vacant Lots"*, used by a variety of governmental agencies including the EPA, U.S. Department of Agriculture, and CDC, has been described as the process of transforming abandoned lots into environmentally friendly ones such as community gardens, parks, and tree farms. Activities involved in "greening" often include initial clearing of debris; break up of soil; planting ground covers, grass, shrubs, and/or trees; and, in some cases, adding fences. It then involves routine maintenance activities such as mowing, pruning, watering and trash removal.

A conceptual framework often used for supporting the greening of vacant lots is the Busy Streets Theory, one that "emerged from the perspective that one way to reduce crime and violence is to generate community connectedness and vibrant neighborhoods that are consistently populated and filled with positive social interactions including neighborly behavior and thriving businesses ... Drawing on ideas from crime prevention through environmental design, community engaged greening not only helps to clean up abandoned properties, demonstrating visual evidence of local care and ownership, but also provides opportunities for positive social interactions among residents."[5]

The Busy Streets Theory is the inspirational framework for this chapter's case example, one that clearly reflects a social marketing approach.

A Social Marketing Approach

Purpose & Focus

This case example is summarized, in part, using an academic study led by the University of Michigan that was conducted over a 5-year timeframe, evaluating the impact of a community-engaged greening program, Clean and Green (C&G), one developed and managed by the Genesee County Land Bank Authority (GLCBA) in Flint, Michigan. Authors of the published study included J. Heinze, A. Krusky-Morey, K. Vagi, T. Reischl, S. Franzen, N. Pruett, R. Cunningham, and M. Zimmerman.[6] The program evaluation objective was to determine whether *Clean and Green parcel sites* contributed to a *reduction in assaults and violent crimes on streets*, by comparing results on similar vacant parcel segments that were left alone.[7]

GCLBA is a "governmental organization formed in 2004 with the mission to restore value to the community be acquiring, developing, and selling vacant and abandoned properties in cooperation with stakeholders who value land ownership. Each year, the GCLBA accepts thousands of properties from the Genesee County Treasurer after tax-foreclosure and the required auctions. Most of the properties have been vacant for years and are now blighted and in need of investment."[8]

Priority Audiences & Desired Behaviors

As with most greening vacant lot programs, residents in the surrounding neighborhood of the GCLBA are the focus for participation in group efforts. In this case in Flint, Michigan, local neighborhood groups are encouraged to *submit a proposal to care for vacant lots in their neighborhood* to the GCLBA. Expected activities, in this case, are focused on *routine maintenance every 3 weeks*, including mowing, weeding, and gardening. A smaller number of the groups studied also engaged in additional activities such as planting a flower or vegetable garden.

GCLBA evaluates applications and selects groups for the upcoming year based on a variety of factors including:[9]

- How strong their connection is to the neighborhood or area in which the vacant lot parcels exist
- Whether or not they express a commitment to engaging youth in the area
- Extent to which they have past experience in similar vacant property maintenance and reuse
- Their capacity, as a group, to care for at least 25 vacant properties every three weeks

A specific audience segment noted that may benefit from this project are youth. Dr. Marc Zimmerman, a research participant in the study, co-director of the institute for Firearm Injury Prevention, and a professor of public health at the University of Michigan where his work has focused on adolescent health commented in "The Academic Minute" that: "My colleagues and I are testing the Busy Streets Theory, which flips the script and explores what it takes to cultivate a safe environment where communities can thrive, and positive social interaction describes the neighborhood. Where youth can grow up in a safe and healthy context where they observe positive behaviors such as neighborliness, experience trust among neighbors, and develop a sense of community where neighbors work together to achieve common goals."[10]

Audience Insights

Barriers to participation may include a lack of belief, even understanding, that greening vacant lots can have an impact on reducing crime. In addition, some will have concerns with the commitment to regular maintenance activities, and whether they have basic skills that will be needed for performance.

Benefits that neighbors value and often experience include gaining a sense of community, collective efficacy, and social control; beautifying of otherwise vacant, littered, and unmaintained properties in their neighborhood; and possibilities that their activities will create a lower neighborhood crime rate.[11]

Motivators include published evidence that their community greening efforts will help reduce violent crime, as well as being offered stipends and provided with necessary tools for maintenance activities.

Key Strategies

As noted, neighborhood groups submit a proposal to care for a vacant lot in their neighborhood. In this Flint, Michigan, case, proposals have opportunities for small amounts of funding to support residents' work. "The Land Bank annually selects community-based organizations for the Clean & Green program through a competitive application process. The number of groups selected depends on annual funding. Each group that is selected to participate is required to maintain at least 25 vacant properties between April and September. Each participating group receives a cash stipend to support its work. The value of the stipend for each group depends on the number of vacant properties the group maintains." [12] Applications are released, including online, in January and are due in February and are selected in March. Starting in May properties are maintained every three weeks and in September property maintenance concludes.

Promotional strategies to inform communities about the program have included active websites, presentations at community group gatherings, news interviews providing testimonials to the program's impact, and online videos portraying groups in action greening the vacant lot.

Program Outputs & Outcomes (2004-2022)

Long term accomplishments for the program overall include the following outputs and outcomes reported by GCLGA in 2022:[13]

- Clean & Green Groups have completed more than 275,000 vacant property mowing's, an estimated $13.7 million value.
- More than 8,200 area residents participated in the program.
- More than 3,575 youth were among participants, and more than 1550 employed area youth.
- GCLBA invested more than $5.8 million directly into community-based organizations through Clean & Green.

In 2021, a story featured by the MILive news network provided an update on a recent greening of vacant lots in the City of Flint reporting that: "Sixty-nine community-based groups signed up to clean and green nearly 3,700 vacant properties in and around the City of Flint every three weeks through September ... Block Clubs, schools, churches, neighborhoods associations, and local nonprofits are some of the many community-based groups participating in the 2021 Clean & Green program." [14] It was further noted that "Ten new groups were selected to participate this season after receiving more applications than ever before. Most of the groups include neighborhood youth, who then create change in their own neighborhoods ... Each group receives a stipend for maintain at least 25 properties every three weeks."[15] A separate news story highlighted that more than 22,000 vacant properties were mowed, and that 500 residents, including 200 youth, were participating in the program.[16]

Evaluation Study Methods & Program Impact

A summary of methods used for the evaluation reported on in the academic study led by the University of Michigan during the 2009-2013 timeframe include the following:

- Flint Police Department recorded and provided police incidence data, ones geo-coded to street segment levels.
- "We compared the incidence of violent crime among 216 residential streets segments in Flint Michigan that contained vacant lots maintained by C&G groups to street segments (n=446) with unmaintained lots. A street segment is a portion of a street with end points either due to a dead-end or intersection with another street. Greening activities occurred from May to September and crime was monitored throughout each season. Street segments in both groups had no vacant lots maintained by C&G groups in the season prior to the season on analysis." [17]

As noted in the introduction to this chapter, the study reported that community-engaged greening of vacant lots is associated with nearly a 40% reduction in assaults and total violent crime compared to vacant lots not maintained by these groups.[18]

Applicable Behavior Change Theories

Perceived Susceptibility[19], a component of the Health Belief Model, is one that may have inspired program planners. It is likely that potential contributors participating in the greening of the vacant lots, and then maintaining them, would be influenced by their perceptions of whether they were personally at risk of being a victim of a violent crime associated with that vacant lot. Sharing evaluation results publicly, ones confirming the correlation with decreased crime, was potentially one strategy that increased participation levels.

Participation in this "hands on" work project was also likely influenced by perceptions of *self-efficacy*[20], one stating that the priority audience needs to believe that "he or she has the skills and abilities necessary for performing the behavior."

The program feature that participants worked in groups, as opposed to on their own, would be supported by the influence of *implicit norms*[21], creating a perception for the behavior to be the norm for a group the participant perceived themselves to be a part of.

Social Marketing Principles Contributing to Success[22]

Several social marketing principles that likely contributed to success include:

- *Audiences selected as a priority*, members of a residential community and often a formal group, were ones that could be identified and reached, and would realize desired benefits.
- *Expected behaviors,* and timing for completions, were made clear.
- In many of the programs, *monetary incentives* were offered.
- Potential program impact, especially in terms of decreased crime, was made *"visible and public."*

References

[1] J. Heinze, et al., "Busy Streets Theory: The Effects of Community-engaged Greening on Violence" *American Journal of Community Psychology* (September 2018), accessed at National Library of Medicine https://www.ncbi.nlm.nih.gov/pmc/articles/PMC6373470/

[2] Ibid.

[3] News Medical Life Sciences, "Vacant lot greening can reduce community-level crime and violence, research shows" (October 2022), accessed at https://www.news-medical.net/news/20221028/Study-Vacant-lot-greening-can-reduce-community-crime-violence.aspx

[4] EPA, "What are Vacant Lots?" (March 2022), accessed at https://www3.epa.gov/region1/eco/uep/vacantlots.html

[5] J. Heinze, et al., "Busy Streets Theory: The Effects of Community-engaged Greening on Violence" *American Journal of Community Psychology* (September 2018), accessed at National Library of Medicine https://www.ncbi.nlm.nih.gov/pmc/articles/PMC6373470/

[6] Ibid.

[7] Ibid.

[8] Genesee County Land Bank, "Who We Are" (n.d.), accessed at https://www.thelandbank.org/whoweare.asp

[9] Genesee County Land Bank, "Community Groups Fighting Blight One Property at a time" (n.d.) , accessed at https://www.thelandbank.org/clean_green_prog.asp

[10] The Academic Minute, "Marc Zimmerman, University of Michigan-Busy Streets Theory" (October 2018), accessed at https://academicminute.org/2018/10/marc-zimmerman-university-of-michigan-busy-streets-theory/

[11] J. Heinze, et al., "Busy Streets Theory: The Effects of Community-engaged Greening on Violence" *American Journal of Community Psychology* (September 2018), accessed at National Library of Medicine https://www.ncbi.nlm.nih.gov/pmc/articles/PMC6373470/

[12] Genesee County Land Bank, "Community Groups Fighting Blight One Property at a time" (n.d.) , accessed at https://www.thelandbank.org/clean_green_prog.asp

[13] Ibid.

[14] Mlive, "Dozens of groups hit the streets to beautify vacant lots in Flint neighborhoods" (May 13, 2021), accessed at https://www.mlive.com/news/flint/2021/05/dozens-of-groups-hit-the-streets-to-beautify-vacant-lots-in-flint-neighborhoods.html

[15] Ibid.

[16] East Village Magazine, "Genesee County Land Bank accepting applications for 2021 Clean & Green season" (February 3, 2021), accessed at https://www.eastvillagemagazine.org/2021/02/03/genesee-county-land-bank-accepting-applications-for-2021-clean-green-season

[17] J. Heinze, et al., "Busy Streets Theory: The Effects of Community-engaged Greening on Violence" *American Journal of Community Psychology* (September 2018), accessed at National Library of Medicine https://www.ncbi.nlm.nih.gov/pmc/articles/PMC6373470/

[18] Ibid.

[19] N. Lee, P. Kotler, and J. Colehour, *Social Marketing: Behavior Change for Good,* 7th Ed. (Thousand Oaks, CA: SAGE, 2024), p.81.

[20] Ibid., p.83.

[21] Ibid., pp.84-86.

[22] N. Lee, P. Kotler, and J. Colehour, *Social Marketing: Behavior Change for Good,* 7th Ed. (Thousand Oaks, CA: SAGE, 2024)

Chapter 13

Communities
Enhancing Street Lighting

Background

This is a second chapter that highlights the potential for reducing gun deaths and injuries using a *physical environmental design* approach, with an intent, in this case, on deterring outdoor and nighttime crime on public streets and properties. This strategy is supported by Behavioral Economics theories emphasizing that even "small changes to the environment can have surprisingly large effects on human behavior."[1] The appeal to cities of making these small changes is, in part, driven by the potential for these interventions to be low cost, and to achieve a high rate of return on investment of resources.

A variety of environmental factors in communities can impact levels of mass shootings and other firearm homicides on public streets, with risk greater in economically disadvantaged neighborhoods,[2] at locations with more bars and restaurants, and on dark streets.[3] Studies included in this chapter suggest, even confirm, that simple modifications to physical space may reduce the likelihood of crime and violence by making it riskier, more difficult, and less rewarding for potential offenders.[4]

A Social Marketing Approach

Purpose & Focus

The social marketing approach presented in this chapter features efforts to *reduce gun deaths and injuries from outdoor and nighttime crime on public streets and properties* is one with a focus on *enhancing street lighting*. A report in 2021 by Everytown for Gun Safety, a U.S. gun prevention organization, emphasizes that "Gun crime benefits from darkness. Poor lighting makes witness identification more difficult and may make residents less likely to report or intervene in crimes. But there is a simple solution to this problem: improve lighting in areas with higher rates of gun crimes."[5]

The U.S. Department of Justice discusses in a guide for improving street lighting that the "effect of enhanced lighting can be attributed to different factors, including increased informal surveillance by neighbors and police presence being more visible to offenders. Moreover, better lighting conditions can also increase community cohesiveness."[6]

Priority Audiences & Desired Behaviors

In most instances, efforts to *enhance street lighting* in high-risk public spaces to deter crime will be led by upstream audiences, agencies such as *city governments*, with support from *local police departments*, *city councils*, and *housing authorities*. Efforts would also benefit from actions of midstream audiences such as *citizens* living in at risk neighborhoods, advocating with upstream decision makers for this protective action. In the end, it is intended that these actions will *deter the downstream audience, potential criminal offenders, from violent crimes.*

Audience Insights

Barriers

Questions and concerns that communities considering enhanced lighting projects are likely to have include:

- Questioning whether this will work
- Concerns for potential complaints and opposition to impact of brighter lights
- Justifying costs for installation and increased energy costs
- Lack of knowledge about options for lighting and how to choose
- Lack of methods to objectively prioritize locations for enhancements
- Potential for displacement of crime to other areas/ neighborhoods
- Whether this might lead to more arrests, and therefore more resource allocations

Desired Benefits

Appealing upside outcomes include:

- Reduced crime in their community
- Less costs than other options such as increased policing
- Community resilience and confidence from feeling more safe
- Potential victims supported to protect themselves

Motivators

The U.S. Department of Justice's guide book on *Improving Street Lighting to Reduce Crime in Residential Areas,* addresses many of these perceived barriers, helps to ensure potential benefits, and is

motivating for those considering enhanced strategies, with one
section of the guide presenting clear rationale in terms of how
improved lighting could reduce crime (See Box 13.1).[7]

"In Darkness

1. Improved lighting deters potential offenders by increasing the
   risk that they will be seen or recognized when committing
   crimes.
2. Police become more visible, thus leading to a decision to desist
   from crime.
3. If improved lighting leads to the arrest and imprisonment of
   repeat offenders, they can no longer commit crimes in the area.
4. New lighting can encourage residents to spend more time on
   their stoops or in their front yards in the evenings and thus
   increase informal surveillance.
5. Improved lighting can encourage more people to walk at
   night, which would increase informal surveillance.

In Daylight

1. New lighting shows that city government and the police are
   determined to control crime. As a result, potential offenders
   might no longer see the neighborhood as affording easy
   pickings. In additions, citizens might be motivated to pass on
   information about offenders.
2. Better lighting can increase community pride and
   cohesiveness, leading to a greater willingness to intervene in
   crime and to report it.
3. If offenders commit crime in both light and darkness,
   nighttime arrests and subsequent imprisonment would
   reduce both daytime and nighttime crime."

Box 13.1 *How Improved Lighting Could REDUCE Crime (Adapted from Pease
1999)*

Source: U.S. Department of Justice, "Improving Street Lighting to Reduce
Crime in Residential Areas" (December 2008), p.6., accessed at Improving

Street Lighting to Reduce Crime in Residential Areas (usdoj.gov). Adapted from Ken Pease (1999) "A Review of Street Lighting Evaluations, Crime Prevention Studies", volume 10).

One strategy to address potential questions and concerns to influence upstream and midstream audiences are the results of studies such as the one presented in the following case example.

Case Example of Enhanced Lighting to Reduce Crime In New York City

Background

In the spring and summer of 2016 in New York City, a rigorous field experiment was conducted to answer the question: "To what extent can changes to the physical environment be successful in reducing crimes, especially crimes involving violence, which drive the majority of the social costs?"[8] Rationale for the study included an objective to confirm that "The substantial geographic concentration of crime, particularly violent crime, suggests that the social and physical features of the urban landscape might potentially play an important role in the crime production function."[9] And given the potential cost of providing enhanced street lighting at scale, the City wanted to launch this pilot study to investigate the extent to which increased lighting would be a cost effective strategy for reducing serious crime.

The intent, methodology and results of the study were published in 2019 by the National Bureau of Economic Research in a paper: "Reducing Crime Through Environmental Design: Evidence From A Randomized Experiment of Street Lighting in New York City." The research team and authors included A. Chalfin, B. Hansen, J. Lerner, and L. Parker. The experiment involved a unique partnership between the New York City Mayor's Office for Criminal

Justice, the New York City Police Department, and the New York City Housing Authority, with an intent to test the effectiveness of enhancing street lights in reducing street crime, especially violent crime.

The team worked closely with the City for nearly two years developing this study, one that chose a focus on violent crime in public housing communities, as these locations were where violent crime was disproportionately high. The study's methodology included randomizing the provision of street lights to the city's public housing developments, where public housing developments at the time were officially home to more than 400,000 New Yorkers.[10]

Behavior Change Intervention Tested

In social marketing terminology, the primary intervention tool was a product, enhanced lighting, one that it was hoped would made it less likely that potential gun shooters would engage in harmful activities. This is similar to a public health campaign that provides accessible and free COVID tests, making it less likely those who test positive will attend public events.

The specific enhancement to street lighting that was tested was that of installing temporary lighting towers (*product*) at public housing developments across NYC, ones described in the published study as very tall and prominent, "extraordinarily luminous", and equipped with "automatic timers that were set to switch on at sunset and off at sunrise."[11]

Methodology

NYPD provided a list of 80 high-priority public housing developments, ones selected based on elevated crime rates, as well as perceived need for additional lighting. This list was then randomly divided into two groups with 40 assigned to the treatment condition sample that would receive new lights, and the other 40 developments assigned to a control condition, receiving no additional outdoor lighting.[12]

Crimes measured were classified as Part I Index Crimes, those *accounting for the vast majority of social costs* and considered the *most serious of crimes*, including murder and non-negligent manslaughter, robbery, felony assault, burglary, grand larceny, and motor vehicle theft. [13] Among these, the most frequent are felony assault and robbery, comprising 72 percent of the index crimes that occur outdoors during nighttime hours, with nighttime described as approximately half an hour after the official sunset, and ending approximately half hour before sunrise.[14] Incident-level data used for tracking was gathered and provided by the NYPD and included the date, time, and type of offense, as well as whether the incident occurred indoors or outdoors.

Results

Authors concluded: "We find evidence that communities that were assigned more lighting experienced sizable reductions in crime ... and led, at a minimum, to a *36 percent reduction in nighttime outdoor index crimes.*"[15]

In terms of cost effectiveness of enhanced lighting relative to costs associated with criminal activity, it was stated that, "Annual costs of providing electricity to the additional lights is expected to be $15,000 per development. Over a ten-year planning horizon, we estimate that this type of lighting upgrade will cost, on average, $200,000 per development annually. Given these annual costs, if the effects of lighting persist, we anticipate that the ratio of benefits to the costs of additional lighting would be approximately 4 to 1."[16]

Additional Experiments & Evaluative Perspectives

A report from Arizona State University included results of an evaluation of eight enhanced street lighting trials in the United States and three from the United Kingdom, and "concluded that improved street lighting led to a *21 percent decrease in crime* compared with comparable control areas."[17]

In a report of the U.S. Department of Justice, it is stated that: "It is clear that reductions in crime can be achieved by improvements in street lighting and that these reductions will be most worthwhile in high-crime neighborhoods. It is also clear that improved lighting can reduce crime during the day and at night. This suggests that improvements to lighting not only act as a situational deterrent to crime, but can also improve local community cohesion and pride, which in turn increases the willingness of residents to intervene in crime or cooperate with the police. Improved lighting will also send a message to potential offenders that the neighborhood no longer offers easy opportunities for crime."[18]

Applicable Behavior Change Theories

The *Social Cognitive Theory*[19] states that the likelihood of taking a particular action will be influenced by beliefs that benefits of performing the behavior will outweigh the costs. In this unique situation, the potential criminal might see that the increased likelihood of getting caught as a result of enhanced visibility from lighting outweighs desired benefits from a shooting or robbery.

As noted, the *Behavioral Economics Framework*[20] is also clearly applicable to this behavior change approach, as it stresses how environmental factors influence personal decisions, in this case the perception that they might be seen and caught in a criminal act.

Social Marketing Principles Contributing to Success[21]

Social marketing principles supportive of this case's environmental design approach include:

- *Highlight the costs of competing behaviors*, in this case making it more likely that potential criminals would see their increased visibility as a result of the "bright lights" as a deterrent.
- Consider a *product that will "help"* the potential audience adopt the desired behavior. In this case the desired behavior was to abstain from criminal acts, with the product, enhanced lighting, making this more likely.
- *Social diffusion* is supported by the fact that the intervention, enhanced lighting at high risk street locations, are likely to be maintained, even expanded, overtime.

References

1 NBER.ORG, © 2019 by Aaron Chalfin, Benjamin Hansen, Jason Lerner, and Lucie Parker, "Reducing Crime Through Environmental Design: Evidence from a Randomized Experiment of Street Lighting in New York City" p.1, accessed at "Reducing Crime Through Environmental Design: Evidence from a Randomized Experiment of Street Lighting in New York City (nber.org).

2 ECONOFACT, "Gun Violence in the U.S." (November 2022), accessed at https://econofact.org/gun-violence-in-the-u-s

3 Newark Public Safety Collaborative, (n.d.), "Can Enhanced LED Street Lighting Contribute to Reduce Violent Crime?" https://newarkcollabo rative.org/blog/can-street-lighting-reduce-crime.

4 John Jay, College of Criminal Justice, "Reducing Violence Without Police: A Review of Research Evidence" (November, 2020), accessed at https://johnjayrec.nyc/2020/11/09/av2020/.

5 EVERYTOWN, "Crime Prevention Through Environmental Design" (April 26, 2021), accessed at Crime Prevention Through Environmental Design | Everytown Support Fund.

6 Newark Public Safety Collaborative, (n.d.), "Can Enhanced LED Street Lighting Contribute to Reduce Violent Crime?" https://newarkcollabo rative.org/blog/can-street-lighting-reduce-crime.

7 U.S. Department of Justice, "Improving Street Lighting to Reduce Crime in Residential Areas" (December 2008) p.6, accessed at Improving Street Lighting to Reduce Crime in Residential Areas (usdoj.gov) .

8 NBER.ORG, © 2019 by Aaron Chalfin, Benjamin Hansen, Jason Lerner, and Lucie Parker, "Reducing Crime Through Environmental Design: Evidence from a Randomized Experiment of Street Lighting in New York City" p.3, accessed at "Reducing Crime Through Environmental Design: Evidence from a Randomized Experiment of Street Lighting in New York City (nber.org).

9 Ibid, p.2.

10 Ibid, p.8.

11 Ibid, p.9.

12 Ibid, p.9.

13 Ibid, p.10.

[14] Ibid, p.11.

[15] Ibid., Abstract

[16] Ibid, p.21.

[17] Arizona State University, "What Do Scientific Evaluations Show" (n.d.), accessed at https://popcenter.asu.edu/content/improving-street-lighting-reduce-crime-residential-areas-page-3.

[18] U.S. Department of Justice, "Improving Street Lighting to Reduce Crime in Residential Areas" (December 2008) (p.35), accessed at Improving Street Lighting to Reduce Crime in Residential Areas (usdoj.gov)

[19] N. Lee, P. Kotler, and J. Colehour, *Social Marketing: Behavior Change for Good,* 7th Ed. (Thousand Oaks, CA: SAGE, 2024) p.83.

[20] Ibid., pp.86-88.

[21] N. Lee, P. Kotler, and J. Colehour, *Social Marketing: Behavior Change for Good,* 7th Ed. (Thousand Oaks, CA: SAGE, 2024)

Chapter 14

Street Outreach Workers
Mediating Conflicts & Preventing
Retaliatory Violence

Background

This chapter highlights a community-based approach to reducing gun deaths and injuries, a strategy that Thomas Abt elaborates on in his book *Bleeding Out*. He states in an article in *The Guardian* in 2019 that a community-based approach has the potential to *"reduce gun violence by 50%* in the U.S.'s 40 most violent cities."[1] Abt, a senior research fellow at the Center for International Development at Harvard University as of 2019, supports this potential impact with several relevant facts related to cities with high rates of violence:[2]

- Shootings are concentrated in small places, not in entire communities or neighborhoods.
- In most cities, it is estimated that only about 4% of city blocks account for 50% of crime.
- For example, in Oakland, California, approximately 60% of murders happen within a network of .3% of the city's population.

Abt's career includes having been a prosecutor in Manhattan, a member of the justice department during the Obama

Administration, and a deputy secretary for public safety in New York Governor Andrew Cuomo's office.[3]

An article by Daniel Webster in *Daedalus* in 2022 titled "Public Health Approaches to Reducing Community Gun Violence" elaborates on Abt's recommended approach. "Abt underscores that approaches to urban gun violence should be *focused, balanced*, and *fair*. Focus is necessary because gun violence is highly concentrated among a very small percentage of the population and highly concentrated spatially even within neighborhoods with high rates of shootings. Balance refers to the use of social services and job opportunities along with effective enforcement that can deter gun violence. Fairness is important not only as a matter of justice, but research shows that compliance with laws and cooperation with law enforcement are highly dependent upon whether individuals view police and prosecutors as legitimate and fair."[4] Webster comments further that addressing violence through a public health lens includes creating "environments less conducive to violence, or ones that facilitate social conditions that constrain violence."[5]

A Social Marketing Approach

Purpose & Focus

The social marketing approach presented in this chapter features efforts to *reduce gun deaths and injuries in cities with high rates of violent crimes* with a focus on *community-driven, evidence-based interventions*. These violence intervention programs identify population segments at the highest risk of crime, including gun violence, and work to reduce incidents through targeted interventions. Three major intervention programs described by Everytown for Gun Safety, a U.S. nonprofit organization, include the following:[6]

- *Street Outreach:* This program is said to employ a public health approach, one with street outreach workers trained to mediate conflicts and prevent retaliatory violence among those at-risk to commit or become victims of gun violence.

- *Group Violence Intervention:* This approach features group meetings where members of violent groups, such as gangs, are gathered to hear from social service organizations, law enforcement and select community members regarding potential harsh consequences to continued violence. They are subsequently offered connections to social services including counseling, financial support, and employment opportunities.

- *Hospital-Based Violence Intervention Programs:* These programs are designed for patients who are victims of violence such as a gunshot wound, and are currently in trauma centers and emergency departments. The intent is to engage and support patients while still in the hospital, reducing chances of retaliation and violent injury recurrence. Services provided include potential for obtaining mental health counseling and financial support.

Street Outreach intervention programs are the focus for the remainder of this chapter, including three case examples.

Priority Audiences & Desired Behaviors

Street outreach programs recruit, train, and support a diverse group of workers to *intervene, mediate disputes, and support people* in the community identified as having the highest risk of engaging in, or becoming victims of, gun violence. To support a deep connection and empathy with those at risk for violence, one ideal group of outreach workers are those with a *personal history with gun violence and/or incarceration* as they can draw on their own lived experiences.[7]

Audience Insights

Barriers

For potential and current street outreach workers, a study by the Institute for Policy Research at Northwestern University, in partnership with the Chicago outreach community, provides major insights related to recruitment and retention of streetworkers.[8] Barriers identified include reluctance and concern with putting themselves back into the violence of the streets, with many traumatized from a prior incident and in need for more access to mental healthcare; perceptions of how low the pay is and currently experiencing difficulty in paying their monthly bills; and a lack of healthy relationships for some in their own life, making it difficult to support others to accomplish this.

Benefits & Motivators

The Council on Criminal Justice recommends that to support outreach workers it is important to provide desired resources in order to do the job properly.

"For years, street outreach workers have worked long hours with little pay, no benefits, and with minimal opportunity for upward mobility or advancement. Additionally, workers have not received sufficient support for addressing the trauma – direct and vicarious – that often comes with the work. That must change. Properly resourcing street outreach means creating viable career pathways over the long term and providing the mental health services needed by those who engage in the work."[9]

Three Case Examples: Background, Interventions, Results

Chicago[10]

CeaseFire is a program that was launched in Chicago in 1999 by the Chicago Project for Violence Prevention at the University of Illinois's Chicago School of Public Health. Of all the program's facets, one described as "most notable" involves hiring "violence interrupters" such as street outreach workers. Outreach workers work alone, or in pairs, cruising the streets at night offering nonviolent alternatives to potential offenders such as gang leaders and street youth, and mediating conflicts in high risk CeaseFire neighborhoods. As noted earlier, many outreach streetworkers are former gang members having served time in prison, increasing perceived empathy and credibility among current gang members.

A program evaluation included process as well as outcome measurements. Process evaluations included interviews with CeaseFire staff, police social service workers and community leaders at 17 sites. Interviews were conducted with 297 gang members and street youth to assess program elements and make any recommended adjusts. Outcome measurements focused on seven sites within the city of Chicago, and "analysis based on 17 years of data showed that, as a direct result of CeaseFire, shootings decreased 16-28 percent in four of the seven sites studied."[11]

New York[12]

In 2010, with funding from the U.S. Department of Justice, New York City launched its first *Cure Violence* program, one that uses a neighborhood-based, public-health approach to interrupt violence. Similar to other street outreach programs, efforts rely on outreach workers to "interrupt violence" in neighborhoods most vulnerable to gun violence. As of 2016, the city's Cure Violence program employed more than 80 front-line workers, ones who participate in a 40-hour training workshop where they learn about conflict mediation, active listening, conflict mediation, suicide prevention and interviewing tactics.[13]

The host organization for one of the Cure Violence programs is **Man Up! Inc.**, one that has received funding including grants from New York State, New York City's Young Men's initiative, and the New York City's Council. A study published in 2017 of one Man Up! effort in East New York, Brooklyn, presents a profile of outreach workers, with almost 66% of participants between the ages of 12 and 25, 90% males, and 94% Black.[14] Approximately half of staff members described themselves as having once belonged to a street group such as a gang, as a formerly incarcerated person, or both.[15] Outreach activities for the street workers average approximately 48 hours per worker per month and involve walking around neighborhoods to keep up with "street lore" and interacting with residents to hear about any possibilities of violence.[16] Their presence certainly didn't go unnoticed, with a survey of young men in the neighborhoods indicating that "80 percent of East New York males ages 18-30 recognized at least one staff member from Man UP!"[17]

Results from data analysis of this effort in East New York, Brooklyn, concluded that gun injuries fell 50 percent, and shooting victimizations fell 15% following the implementation of the program.[18] Attitudinal outcomes were also significant. "Young men living in neighborhoods with Cure Violence programs reported sharper reductions in their willingness to use violence compared with young men in similar areas without programs."[19]

Los Angeles

Thomas Abt noted in his article in *The Guardian* in 2019 that a street outreach program in Los Angeles may be one of the best among cities, due, in part, to efforts making it a central part of the city's official response to violence.[20] A study between 2014 and 2015 estimated that Los Angeles's outreach program prevented an estimated 185 violent crimes, including 10 homicides.[21]

The Urban Peace Institute describes the approach in of the Los Angeles Violence Intervention Coalition as "comprised of 16 frontline violence intervention organizations and advocacy groups focused on ending the gun homicide epidemic in Los Angeles. Urban Peace Institute convenes the Los Angeles Violence Intervention Coalition, and is a recognized leader in the field of community safety, just policing and systems reform to end violence and mass incarceration." [22]

The Council on Criminal Justice recommends that street outreach programs follow the Los Angeles model, as it takes some of the street outreach burden off a single provider by funding multiple organizations being trained and organized centrally and working in partnership with local governmental organizations.

It is noted, and should be taken into consideration when developing and funding these programs, that in 2021 several advocacy efforts were being made in Los Angeles to strengthen the program by increasing wages for the street workers. A news article of Trace.org makes it real, describing the life of one worker who "having just completed a prison stint in 2013, she began volunteering as a violence interrupter. She was deployed to mediate street conflicts before they escalated to gunfire. Eventually, a paid position came up, and she took it. Her pay was $16.80 an hour. A mother of five, she had to take a second job cleaning a women's gym at night, which she juggled with college classes."[23]

Recent Governmental Response

In April of 2021, President Biden announced the launch of the *Community Based Violence Intervention and Prevention Initiative*, one the U.S. Department of Justice describes as an "evidence-based violence intervention program based on partnerships among community residents, local government agencies, victim service providers, community-based organizations, law enforcement, hospitals, researchers, and other community stakeholders."[24] The intent is to support a collaborative approach to "help ensure jurisdictions have access to expertise and resources to address community violence."[25]

And in December of 2022, it was reported in a POLITICO news article that "For a year and a half, city and county leaders around the country have received funding, training, and technical assistance, and met regularly with White House officials to bolster community violence intervention programs that have been shown to break cycles of violence ... These programs often connect former gang members and other high-risk individuals with mental health care and other social services." [26]

Applicable Behavior Change Theories

Relative to success in interventions with potential offenders, the *Stages of Change Model* is applicable to this approach given the strategy of focusing on prevention by identifying and having influential conversations with potential offenders when in a state of contemplation, prior to action. [27]

Relative to both outreach workers as well as potential offenders, the *Social Cognitive Theory* is applicable to this program's success, given it states that the likelihood of engaging in a behavior is influenced by whether or not perceived potential benefits from engaging in a behavior will outweigh potential costs. [28] For street outreach workers the potential benefit of preventing violent attacks certainly taps their desire to prevent others from carrying out violent attacks, as well as experiencing the tough times that had lived in the past. And for the potential offenders, the intervention of the street outreach workers emphasizes and makes real the consequences they would experience if they carried through with their intentions to harm.

Social Marketing Principles Contributing to Success[29]

Social marketing principles supportive of this case's environmental design approach include:

- Perhaps the strongest principle this street outreach workers approach employs is that of using *trusted, credible messengers*. It is clear that street workers who have experienced incarceration in the past would not only be able to listen with empathy to stories on the street, but they would also be perceived by the potential offenders as ones "who know what they are talking about."
- Reducing barriers to open communications by having outreach workers *engage in conversations in community neighborhoods*, rather than at an intimidating location such as police station.
- Certainly, the principle of *interventions taking place at points-of-decision making*, in this case with outreach workers walking and talking on the streets and in neighborhoods of violent crimes, was key to reaching priority segments, as well as supporting open and in-depth conversations.

References

[1] The Guardian, T. Abt, "My eight-year plan to dramatically reduce urban gun violence", (December 2019), p.2, accessed at https://www.theguardian.com/us-news/2019/dec/10/us-gun-violence-thomas-abt.

[2] Ibid., p.2.

[3] WIKIPEDIA, "Thomas Abt" (December 20220< accessed at https://en.wiki pedia.org/wiki/Thomas_Abt.

[4] *Daedalus*, D. Webster, "Public Health Approaches to Reducing Community Gun Violence", (January 1, 2022), accessed at https://direct.mit.edu/daed/article/151/1/38/108863/Public-Health-Approaches-to-Reducing-Community-Gun.

[5] Ibid.

[6] EVERYTOWN FOR GUN SAFETY, "Violence Intervention Programs" (2023), accessed at https://www.everytown.org/solutions/violence-intervention-programs/.

[7] Council on Criminal Justice, "Meeting Bulletin #4: Community Based Responses to Violence" (October 2021), accessed at https://counciloncj.org/meeting-bulletin-4-community-based-responses/#.

[8] Northwestern Institute for Policy Research, "The Science and Practice of Street Outreach in Illinois" (December 14, 2021), accessed at https://www.ipr.northwestern.edu/news/2021/n3-symposium-on-street-outreach.html

[9] Council on Criminal Justice, "Meeting Bulletin #4: Community Based Responses to Violence" (October 2021), accessed at https://counciloncj.org/meeting-bulletin-4-community-based-responses/#.

[10] National Institute of Justice, "CeaseFire:A Public Health Approach to Reduce Shootings and Killings" (October 2009), accessed at https://nij.ojp.gov/topics/articles/ceasefire-public-health-approach-reduce-shootings-and-killings.

[11] Ibid.

[12] S. Delgado, L. Alsabahi, K. Wolff, N. Alexander, P. Cobar, J. Butts, CUNY Academic Works, "The Effects of Cure Violence in The South Bronx and East New York, Brooklyn (2017), accessed at https://academicworks.cuny.edu/cgi/viewcontent.cgi?article=1436&context=jj_pubs.

[13] Ibid., p.2.

[14] Ibid., p.2.

[15] Ibid., p.2

[16] Ibid., p.3.

[17] Ibid., p.3.

[18] Ibid., pp.10-11.

[19] Ibid., p.7.

[20] The Guardian, T. Abt, "My eight-year plan to dramatically reduce urban gun violence" (December 2019), accessed at https://www.theguardian.com/us-news/2019/dec/10/us-gun-violence-thomas-abt.

[20] Ibid.

[21] Ibid.

[22] Urban Peace Institute, "LA Violence Intervention Coalition's $400M Call to #FundPeacemakers" (n.d.), accessed at https://www.urbanpeaceinstitute.org/la-intervention-coalition .

[23] The Trace, "The Push to Pay Violence Interrupters a Living Wage" (March 2021), accessed at https://www.thetrace.org/2021/03/gun-violence-interruptor-pay-los-angeles-milwaukee-chicago//

[24] U.S. Department of Justice, "Community Based Violence Intervention and Prevention Initiative" (May 2022), accessed at https://www.ojp.gov/program/cvipi.

[25] Ibid.

[26] POLITICO, "Inside the White House gun violence initiative they say is actually working" (December 2022), accessed at https://www.politico.com/news/2022/12/06/guns-community-violence-intervention-collaborative-00072630.

[27] N. Lee, P. Kotler, and J. Colehour, *Social Marketing: Behavior Change for Good,* 7th Ed. (Thousand Oaks, CA: SAGE, 2024), p.78.

[28] N. Lee, P. Kotler, and J. Colehour, *Social Marketing: Behavior Change for Good,* 7th Ed. (Thousand Oaks, CA: SAGE, 2024), p.83.

[29] N. Lee, P. Kotler, and J. Colehour, *Social Marketing: Behavior Change for Good,* 7th Ed. (Thousand Oaks, CA: SAGE, 2024)

Chapter 15

Citizens
Advocating for Change

Background

In 2021, a Pew Research Center article, *Amid a Series of Mass Shootings in the U.S., Gun Policy Remains Deeply Divisive*,[1] elaborated on the political divide related to gun control measures, especially those with strong public support:

"In an era marked by deep divisions between Republicans and Democrats, few issues are as politically polarizing as gun policy. While a few specific policy proposals continue to garner bipartisan support, the partisan divisions on other proposals-and even on whether gun violence is a serious national problem-have grown wider over the last few years ...

Overall, several gun policy proposals continue to draw broad support from Americans. Nearly nine-in-ten (87%) favor preventing people with mental illnesses from purchasing guns, while 81% favor subjecting private gun sales and sales at gun shows to background checks. Smaller though still sizeable majorities of American support the creation of a federal database tracking all gun sales (66%), and bans on high capacity magazines (64%) and assault-style weapons (63%)."[2]

This chapter highlights a strategy to influence gun policy changes by increasing the awareness and understanding among elected officials of the current and actual high levels of public support for laws and policies intended to reduce gun deaths and injuries.

A Social Marketing Approach

Purpose & Focus

On December 15, 2012, one day after the Sandy Hook School shooting in Newtown, Connecticut, Shannon Watts, a mother of five and a gun violence prevention activist, launched a Facebook page that grew into a grassroots movement, one branded *Moms Demand Action* (MDA).[3] The organization has been on a mission for more than 10 years (as of 2023) to reduce gun violence by *influencing elected officials to "pass common sense laws and policies to make our country safer"* [4], especially those with strong public support. Relative to the social marketing framework, elected officials are the priority audience, and citizen advocacy is the focus.

Priority Audiences & Desired Behaviors

One of the priority elected official groups for most gun-related advocacy groups are *state legislators,* an audience often perceived as most influenced by their constituents, and more able and likely to pass legislation at a state and local level. Strategies employed by a variety of advocacy groups to influence this audience focus on persuading these elected officials to *support major gun-related legislative measures that have strong public support* (behavior) including ones related to:

- New or Revised Laws/Bills/Regulations (e.g., firearm permitting laws)

- Increased Funding (e.g., to support community violence intervention programs)
- New or Revised Regulations (e.g., requiring gun dealers to post signage with specific language about public health risks associated with unsecured firearms)
- Dissemination of Information/Education (e.g., prime options for safe gun storage)

Audience Insights

Barriers

In the wake of the school mass shooting at Robb Elementary School in Parkland, Florida, in 2018, an ABC News special highlighted "5 Common Reasons Lawmakers Don't Change Gun Laws", with content based on polls, roundtable discussions, secondary research and personal interviews.[5] The top five included:

- *"It's not about guns-it's about mental health."* Proponents advocate for support and funding for better mental-health monitoring and treatment versus increased gun control.
- *"If a bad guy wants a gun, they'll find a way to get it."* This is backed by facts such as the U.S. having the highest number of civilian firearms per capita, providing "so many guns already on the street."[6]
- *"It's too soon to politicize this tragedy."* It was noted that some lawmakers express reluctance to address more gun-related legislation in the immediate aftermath of gun-related tragedies, citing it as being insensitive to victims and their families.
- *"Schools have the "option" to arm teachers."* Some suggest that in some cases increased security at school locations is what is needed and should be the focus.

- *"What about the Second Amendment?"* Too much restriction to gun ownership would infringe on the "right to bear arms."[7]

In addition, those reluctant to support new legislation are likely to have concerns with disapproval among their constituents and colleagues, as well as pushback from gun lobbies.

Desired Benefits & Motivators

Certainly, believing that the proposed legislative changes would *save lives* would be one of the major reasons for supporting proposed actions, highlighting the need for facts regarding what impact proposed changes would have on reducing gun deaths and injuries.

Believing that their support for change would increase chances of being reelected is also a major motivating factor. It is likely that legislators will be most inspired to support what their constituents approve and disapprove of. Even though some proposed legislation has broad public support, it might not be strongly supported by the constituents in their district, but if they learned of strong support, it would be motivating.

Key Strategies

Products: As noted earlier, the grassroots movement MDA works, in part, to influence state legislators to support specific proposed legislative actions that have strong public support. For this case, the more specific actions advocated for by MDA volunteers can be thought of as *products* and include proposed *specific new or revised laws, bills, regulations,* and *programs for increased funding*. This is similar to an effort to increase eating of healthy foods, with fruits and vegetables an example of products being promoted in some campaigns. Additional tangible goods to support these legislative "purchases" often feature documents to increase their knowledge and understanding including relevant fact sheets, draft copies of proposed changes, and current data on public support.

Price: MDA praises legislators (a nonmonetary incentive) who support proposed changes in a variety of formats including posting regular updates on their website featuring lawmakers who were successful in getting legislation passed in their state.[8] In addition, MDA supports legislative candidates, ones referred to as "Gun sense candidates", who have advocated for reform, helping to increase their visibility and support among voters. In fact, in 2022, 279 MDA volunteers ran for office in 42 states, with 86 percent of them women, and half of those who ran won their races.[9]

Place: MDA has volunteer chapters in every state and within those chapters, there are hundreds of local groups, ones that can advocate with elected officials in their state's legislature, often in person.[10]

Promotion: MDA's promotional strategies focus on supporting volunteer efforts to reach and influence their state legislators.

Messages: Relative to a proposed bill/law/regulation/increased funding, MAD highlights *facts on why it should be supported.* Volunteer advocates can access the downloadable app *Demand Action* that provides information they can access to use in their communications with legislators. Persuasive information may include levels of support among their constituents, examples of support in other states for similar actions, as well as potential for reduction in gun deaths and injuries.

Messengers: Primary messengers are those advocating with state legislators and are *MDA volunteers.* Although MDA was founded by mothers, similar to the founding of *Mothers Against Drunk Driving*, many volunteers are dads and citizens who do not have children. Over the years, outreach for volunteers has expanded to students in high schools and colleges and communities across the country. Messengers are recruited through social networks of current volunteers, on websites and using social media including an MDA Facebook page to learn about upcoming events and local groups that potential volunteers can join.

Communication Channels: MDA, and its volunteers, communicate to legislators through a variety of channels including social media, organized events such as National Advocacy Day, phone calls, signing of petitions, marches, attending legislative sessions, and offering testimonials. MDA's website includes gun violence statistics by state, offering elected officials easy access to data for their state relative to others.

Creative Elements: The MOMS DEMAND ACTION for Gun Sense in America brand and slogan is still in use in 2023, more than 10 years since launch in 2012. To increase visibility and recognition of volunteers at public events, as stated on their website, "We're the ones in the red shirts." Websites and materials feature graphics and copy using vivid red, white, and blue colors, and include numerous photographs of volunteers in action at marches and signing petitions, and videos of advocates giving testimonials at legislative sessions.[11]

Results

As of 2023, MDA has a chapter in every state and nearly 10 million supporters.[12] Legislative victories reported by MDA include ones listed in Table 15.1, ones that represent a variety of measures volunteers have advocated for at the state level.

Type of Measure	State & Date Passed	Measures that Mda considered victories Ones influenced in part By State Legislators
Laws & Bills & Ordinances	New York July 2022	New York Governor and New York Legislature approve measure to strengthen New Yor's *concealed carry permitting process.*
	New Jersey July 2022	New Jersey Governor signs into law measures to close loopholes for importing *out-of-state firearms*, and strengthening the state's *firearm permitting laws.*
	Delaware June 2022	Governor signs into a law a comprehensive package of *gun safety bills.*
	Illinois May 2022	Governor signs House Bill legislation to address the threat of *ghost guns.*
	Nebraska April 2022	Nebraska lawmakers *reject permitless carry.*
	Maryland April 2022	Governor announces he will allow a bill prohibiting sale or possession of *ghost guns* to become law.
	Colorado March 2022	Governor signs house Bill "The Vote Without Fear Act" that *prohibits the open carry of firearms near polling and other electoral locations.*
	Washington State March 2022	Governor signs three gun safety bills into law including:[13] 1. Where guns can be carried, including *prohibiting carry guns at schools, local government meetings and election-related facilities* 2. How *firearms without serial numbers will be handled* 3. Kinds of *magazines* that can be made and sold

Type of Measure	State & Date Passed	Measures that Mda considered victories Ones influenced in part By State Legislators
	Illinois March 2022	House of Representatives passes legislation that would require the State Department of Public Health to develop and implement a two-year statewide *safe gun storage campaign.*
	Indiana February 2022	Senate Judiciary Committee amends House bill to include policies that would require an individual to obtain a *provisional handgun license* while waiting for a traditional handgun license, with the provisional license including a background check.
RESOLUTIONS	Ohio April 2022	Cincinnati Public Schools Board of Education passes a resolution to distribute information on the Be SMART program educating parents and gun owners about the importance of *secure firearm storage.*
FUNDING	New Mexico March 2022	New Mexico legislature allocates $9 million for violence intervention programs.
	Oregon May 2022	Portland Mayor includes over $10 million for *violence intervention programs* in city budget proposal.
	Connecticut May 2022	Lawmakers approve new state budget that includes millions for funding gun violence prevention.

Table 15.1 *Examples of State Measures Passed in 2022 & Considered Victories by MAD in 2022*[14]

Applicable Behavior Change Theories

The *Exchange Theory*, which emphasizes that behaviors are more likely to be adopted when perceived benefits outweigh perceived costs, clearly contributed to the success of MDA advocates. [15] By consistently presenting to elected officials the levels of support that their constituents have for proposed legislation, and the number of gun-related deaths and injuries that could be reduced, support for change was more likely.

MDA advocates were also able to motivate support for change by leveraging the *Theory of Reasoned Action/Theory of Planned Behavior* one that highlights the best predictor of behavior is intention to act, which is influenced, in part, by perceived social norms. [16], With advocates making themselves highly visible, most often in citizen groups, perceptions of public support for proposed measures was strengthened.

Social Marketing Principles Contributing to Success[17]

Several social marketing principles employed by MAD are applicable:

- *Highlighting the costs of competing behaviors*, in this case presenting facts to legislators regarding the number of gun-related deaths and injuries that could be attributed to existing laws and policies (e.g., the number of deaths at mass shootings where high-capacity magazines were used)
- *Bringing benefits of a desired behavior to the present*, with advocates also emphasizing the current levels of public support among their constituents for a proposed legislation
- *Taking advantage of prior and existing similar efforts*, with information disseminated by MDA on examples in other states where a similar measure had been adopted

- *Delivering messages at points of decision-making,* in this case with advocates gathering at state legislative facilities and meeting with legislators currently considering proposed legislation reform
- *Providing valued nonmonetary incentives,* including recognition in a variety of highly visible media channels for legislators who supported reform

References

[1] Pew Research Center, "Amid a Series of Mass Shootings in the U.S., Gun Policy Remains Deeply Divisive" (April 2021), accessed at Amid a Series of Mass Shootings in the U.S., Gun Policy Remains Deeply Divisive | Pew Research Center

[2] Ibid.

[3] MOMS DEMAND ACTION, "Meet Shannon Watts, Founder of Moms Demand Action" (n.d.), accessed at Meet Shannon Watts, Founder of Moms Demand Action - Moms Demand Action | Moms Demand Action

[4] MOMS DEMAND ACTION, "Our Victories" (2022), accessed at https://momsdemandaction.org/about/victories/

[5] ABC NEWS, "5 common reasons lawmakers don't change gun laws" (February 21, 2018), accessed at https://abcnews.go.com/Politics/common-reasons-lawmakers-change-gun-laws/story?id=53142420

[6] Ibid.

[7] Ibid.

[8] MOMS DEMAND ACTION, "Our Victories" (2022), accessed at https://momsdemandaction.org/about/victories/

[9] 19th News.org "10 years after Sandy Hook, Moms Demand Action volunteers are turning activism into political power" (December 14, 2022), accessed at https://19thnews.org/2022/12/moms-demand-action-gun-control-elected-office/

[10] MOMS DEMAND ACTION, "Our Story" (2022), accessed at https://momsdemandaction.org/about/

[11] MOMS DEMAND ACTION, "Together, we will end gun violence." (n.d.), accessed at Home - Moms Demand Action | Moms Demand Action

[12] MOMS DEMAND ACTION, "Our Story" (2022), accessed at https://momsdemandaction.org/about/

[13] The Spokesman-Review, "Inslee signs Washington State gun regulations into law." (March 2022), accessed at https://www.spokesman.com/stories/2022/mar/23/inslee-signs-gun-regulations-into-law-heres-how-th/

[14] MOMS DEMAND ACTION, "Our Victories" (2022), accessed at https://momsdemandaction.org/about/victories/

[15] N. Lee, P. Kotler, and J. Colehour, *Social Marketing: Behavior Change for Good*, 7th Ed. (Thousand Oaks, CA: SAGE, 2024), p.90.

[16] N. Lee, P. Kotler, and J. Colehour, *Social Marketing: Behavior Change for Good,* 7th Ed. (Thousand Oaks, CA: SAGE, 2024), p.82.

[17] N. Lee, P. Kotler, and J. Colehour, *Social Marketing: Behavior Change for Good,* 7th Ed. (Thousand Oaks, CA: SAGE, 2024)

Chapter 16

Potential Victims of Domestic Violence Homicides
Getting Help from Mobile Apps

Background

Domestic violence is noted by the Johns Hopkins Center for Gun Violence Solutions as a public health crisis in the U.S., and is described as "a pattern of verbal, physical, emotional, and/or sexual abuse in any relationship that is used by a partner to gain or maintain power and control over the other partner."[1]

This chapter highlights a social marketing strategy designed to address concerning statistics regarding domestic violence homicides in the U.S., ones that substantiate the need for a focus on potential women victims, and the use of guns as a weapon:

- "Every month, an average of 57 women are killed with a firearm by an intimate partner."[2] This equates to an average of almost two every day.
- "Nearly half of all women killed in the U.S. are murdered by a current or former intimate partner."[3]
- "More than half of these intimate partner homicides are committed with guns."[4]
- "Female intimate partners are far more likely to be the victims of violent crimes committed by intimate partners than men."[5]

What is Known About the Women Victims?

- The average age of female homicide victims is 41 years old (2018).[6]
- In terms of race, young, racial/ethnic minority women are disproportionately affected. CDC emphasizes that these racial differences underscore the importance of prioritizing intervention efforts to populations most at risk.[7]

What is Known About These Offenders?

- For homicides in which the victim to offender relationship could be identified, 92 percent of female victims were murdered by a male they knew.[8]
- For victims who knew their offenders, 63 percent of female homicide victims were wives or intimate acquaintances of their killers.[9]
- One in depth research study on domestic homicide cases included interviews with killers and emphasized that: "Those who commit violence share a common need to be in control, and instead of occurring spontaneously, the act is, in fact, usually premeditated." [10]

What are Factors that put Potential Victims at Risk and What Factors are Protective?

CDC sees intimate partner violence as preventable,[11] and encourages increased awareness and understanding of factors that put potential victims at risk, as well as those that can provide protection. They note that the following should be considered contributing factors, but may not be causal factors:[12]

- Risk Factors include a combination of *individual factors* (e.g., low self-esteem, low income); *relationship factors* (e.g., dominance of the relationship by one partner over the other); *community factors* (e.g., communities with high rates of violence and crime); and *societal factors* (e.g., traditional gender norms and inequality).

- Protective Factors include a combination of *relationship factors* (e.g., strong support networks), and *community factors* (e.g., feeling connected and involved in the community; coordination of services among community agencies; and access to safe housing, mental health services, and financial aid).

What are Some of the Related Policy Changes that are Being Proposed?

Although this book focuses on individual voluntary behavior change strategies to address social issues such as gun violence, it is worth noting a few policy change recommendations related to this case purpose and focus. Several recommended by the Johns Hopkins Center for Gun Violence Solutions would prohibit the following individuals from purchasing and possessing firearms: [13]

- Those convicted of misdemeanor crimes of domestic violence
- Those subject to domestic violence protective orders
- Those convicted of a misdemeanor crime of stalking

What are Recommended Community-Based Strategies to Reduce Domestic Violence?

CDC suggests six strategies to address this public health crisis:

1. "Teach safe and healthy relationship skills.
2. Engage influential adults and peers.

3. Disrupt the developmental pathways toward partner violence.
4. Create protective environments.
5. Strengthen economic supports for families.
6. Support survivors to increase safety and lessen harms. "[14]

This chapter highlights a social marketing effort most related to the sixth strategy recommended by CDC, one to increase safety and lessen harm among potential victims, as well as survivors.

A Social Marketing Approach

Purpose & Focus

The social marketing approach presented in this chapter features efforts to *reduce gun deaths and injuries among females experiencing domestic violence* with a focus on *increasing their access to timely interventions*. It is noted that this focus on timely interventions is grounded in the perspective that domestic abuse should be seen as a red flag for potential domestic homicide, [15] and that strategies are needed to disrupt this cycle of events.

Priority Audiences & Desired Behavior

As noted, *females experiencing domestic abuse* are the priority audience for this case example. Relevant findings in a CDC national survey indicate that, nationally, one in three women (ages 18+) experience severe intimate partner violence (IPV).[16] Forms of domestic abuse by a current or former partner or spouse include patterns of verbal, physical, emotional, and/or sexual abuse, as well as stalking. The major strategy to be highlighted in this chapter is one especially designed to assist those who have not been reaching out to others regarding their abuse, and have not been documenting their experiences. It is also intended to capture the attention of women who have just left their abusive partners, as this can be one of the most dangerous "moments in time."

The intended behavior outcome is for these women experiencing domestic abuse to *download and utilize a recommended app,* one customed designed to provide a variety of resources that could prevent escalation of abuse to homicide.

Audience Insights

Barriers

Situations and concerns that might prevent the use of these apps include:

- Fear that the intimate partner will find out and escalate abusive behaviors, since abusive partners often closely monitor their victim's phone activity
- Embarrassment when others find out they are involved in an abusive relationship like this
- Disclosing that a once-loving partner has become abusive
- Concern whether the app might be difficult to use, especially in emergency situations
- Lack of awareness that the app exists and how to access it

Desired Benefits

What would be seen as "worth the trouble of accessing an app", and the vulnerability from "reaching out to others", is the belief that this app, and the resources offered by it, will *help reduce, even stop, further abuse, including homicide.*

Motivators

Given the barriers and desired benefits, it would be motivating to access the app if these potential users learned that:

- There are tactics/devices on apps that will secure information that you provide, such as having passwords be protected and providing options for icons for the app on your phone's display that make it unrecognizable to others.
- Similar to most mobile apps, most relevant apps are free, and easy to find and download.
- The apps have been developed and/or supported by organizations nationwide with experience in assisting women victims of domestic violence.
- The apps provide a variety of options for local contacts and resources to reach out to for help.
- Information is provided on apps that includes tips on what you can do to reduce escalation of abuse.
- One section of some apps is for you to enter and safely store incidents of abuse, ones that may be of use if and when there are any criminal charges in the future.

Key Strategies

One of the first and largest online and mobile searchable directory of domestic violence programs and shelters in the U.S. is Domestic Shelter, an organization launched in 2014 that is provided for and operated by Alliance for HOPE International.[17] It is considered to be a leading source of free and helpful tools and information for those experiencing domestic violence, including offerings of mobile apps. Efforts focus on increasing awareness of services available for those experiencing domestic violence that make it fast and easy for victims, as well as their friends and family, to document violent incidents, seek immediate help, and find services and information best suited to their location, language and other needs.[18]

In 2023, Domestic Shelters participated in a partnership to launch a U.S. version of *Bright Sky*, one of the latest digital resources for those concerned about domestic violence. At the time, the app, which had launched in 2018, was available in 13 countries. *Bright Sky* can be downloaded onto mobile phones and enables users to:

- "Identify the types and signs of domestic violence
- Assess the safety of their relationship or that of a friend or loved one
- Access information about different forms of abuse and how to help a friend that may be affected
- Locate local resources and support services." [19]

Domestic Shelter's CEO & President of Theresa's Fund and DomesticShelters.org, Ashley Rumschlag, shared that at the time of this app's launch in the U.S, "Experiencing abuse isn't something that is easy to open up about, and technology has the potential to create a safe place where people can get answers to their questions when they don't feel comfortable reaching out to friends and family or a trained Domestic Violence advocate."[20]

Additional apps that Domestic Shelter notes on their website are ones that address a variety of major concerns with using an app related to domestic violence, as well as provide unique features such as timely intervention tools, words of advice, and convenient access to resources. A few of those noted as examples of the variety of features available are described below, including the first one, *Aspire,* that reported, as of 2015, more than 100,00 downloads:[21]

- ***To Help Your Information Be Secure****: Aspire,* at first glance looking like a simple news feed, making it less likely an abusive partner will explore input on the app, also providing access to trusted contacts including family and friends

- *To Keep a Log of Abusive Incidents*: *VictimsVoice PWA*, helping users to create records of abuse on iPhones or iPads, ones that can then be legally admissible in court
- *To Record Sounds in the Room*: *Rev Voice Recorder and Memos*, providing a means to record an abuser's threats as well as sounds of physical abuse occurring
- *To Record a Phone Call*: *TapeaCall Pro.*, supporting the recording of incoming and outgoing calls without the third party knowing
- *To Help Recognize an Abuser*: *RUSafe App*, helping users decide if they are possibly in a dangerous situation with a potential abuser

The Bright Sky app is promoted in a variety of ways including social media campaigns, paid search/display ads, events (webinars and in-person), email campaigns and PR.

Applicable Behavior Change Theories

This case clearly illustrates the benefits of addressing conditions that impact the likelihood of behavior change, ones central to *The Health Belief Model*.[22] This behavior change theory emphasizes key factors that influence whether or not an individual is likely to undertake a recommended preventive action, in this chapter's case example, that of using an app to help reduce chances of domestic homicide. Four of the major factors that The Health Belief Model calls out are listed below, and are illustrated by strategies used in this chapter's case example:

- *Perceived Susceptibility*: Apps provide information, including warning signs, that help determine if what is being experienced is domestic violence.

- *Perceived Severity*: Several components of the apps emphasize the likelihood that current forms of abuse including verbal, physical, and/or sexual abuse are red flags that this may escalate to a homicide.
- *Perceived Benefits of Taking Action:* Messages emphasize that reaching out for help to family/ friends, and credible community and professional resources may deter the homicide, as well as help disrupt current incidents of abuse.
- *Perceived Barriers to Taking Action:* Several app features reduce major barriers including: icons that don't suggest the app is one related to domestic violence; most apps being free and easily downloaded; and information on apps being secured with passwords.

Social Marketing Principles Contributing to Success[23]

A strong social marketing principle is to consider all 4P intervention tools to address barriers and provide desired benefits. This is apparent in program offerings:

- *Products to Help* (e.g., apps with features that can be tailored to unique situations and provide resources relevant to issues currently being experienced)
- *Price Incentives* (e.g., most apps are free, and provide anonymity)
- *Place Options* (e.g., apps are simple to download from a variety of sources)
- *Promotion Messages* (e.g., stories of victims that were helped by the app)

In addition, *partnerships* with national and local organizations pooling resources provides economic efficiencies for programs, as well as a variety of trusted services.

References

[1] EFSBV, "Domestic Violence and Firearms" (July 2020), accessed at https://efsgv.org/learn/type-of-gun-violence/domestic-violence-and-firearms/

[2] CAP, "Guns and Violence Against Women" (January 2022), accessed at https://www.americanprogress.org/article/guns-and-violence-against-women/

[3] EFSBV, "Domestic Violence and Firearms" (July 2020), accessed at https://efsgv.org/learn/type-of-gun-violence/domestic-violence-and-firearms/

[4] Ibid.

[5] Violence Policy Center, "When Men Murder Women" (2023), accessed at https://vpc.org/when-men-murder-women-introduction/

[6] Ibid. Section One. National Data

[7] CDC, "Morbidity and Mortality Weekly Report" (July 2017), accessed at https://www.cdc.gov/mmwr/volumes/66/wr/mm6628a1.htm

[8] Violence Policy Center, "When Men Murder Women" (2023), accessed at https://vpc.org/when-men-murder-women-introduction/

[9] Ibid.

[10] H. Reese, JSTOR DAILY, "Ending the Myths about Domestic Homicide" (September 2021), accessed at https://daily.jstor.org/ending-myths-domestic-homicide/

[11] CDC, "Fast Facts" (October 2022), accessed at Fast Facts: Preventing Intimate Partner Violence | Violence Prevention | Injury Center | CDC

[12] CDC, "Violence Prevention: Risk and Protective Factors" (2022), Risk and Protective Factors | Intimate Partner Violence | Violence Prevention | Injury Center | CDC

[13] EFSBV, "Domestic Violence and Firearms: Recommendations" (July 2020), accessed at https://efsgv.org/learn/type-of-gun-violence/domestic-violence-and-firearms/

[14] CDC, "Violence Prevention: Intimate Partner Violence" (November 2021), accessed at https://www.cdc.gov/violenceprevention/intimatepartnerviolence/prevention.html

15 H. Reese, JSTOR DAILY, "Ending the Myths about Domestic Homicide" (September 2021), accessed at https://daily.jstor.org/ending-myths-domestic-homicide/

16 CDC, "The National Intimate Partner and Sexual Violence Survey: 2016/2017 Report" (October 2022) p.3, accessed at https://www.cdc.gov/violenceprevention/pdf/nisvs/NISVSReportonIPV_2022.pdf

17 Domesticshelters.org, "About DomesticShelters.org" (n.d.), accessed at https://www.domesticshelters.org/about

18 Ibid.

19 Domesticshelters.org, "Life Saving App Supports Millions Affected by DV" (2023), accessed at Life-Saving App Supports Millions Affected by DV (domesticshelters.org)

20 Ibid.

21 Domesticshelters.org, "Apps That Could Help Save Your Life" (July 2015), accessed at Apps That Could Help Save Your Life (domesticshelters.org) and Domesticshelters.org, "Lifesaving Apps for Survivors of Domestic Violence" (July 2020), accessed at https://www.domesticshelters.org/articles/technology/lifesaving-apps-for-survivors-of-domestic-violence

22 N. Lee, P. Kotler, and J. Colehour, *Social Marketing: Behavior Change for Good,* 7th Ed. (Thousand Oaks, CA: SAGE, 2024), pp. 80-83.

23 N. Lee, P. Kotler, and J. Colehour, *Social Marketing: Behavior Change for Good,* 7th Ed. (Thousand Oaks, CA: SAGE, 2024)

Chapter 17

Citizens Who See Something Suspicious Say Something

Background: The See Something, Say Something Program

Shortly after the September 11, 2001, terrorist attack, the New York Metropolitan Transportation Authority (MTA) implemented and trademarked the slogan *"If You See Something, Say Something®"*, inspired by evidence overtime that potential perpetrators most often follow a discernible planning process.[1] As described in an article by Stratfor Worldview on the Center for The National Interest's website, potential perpetrators most often "identify their target, plan out how they will conduct the attack, conduct surveillance and acquire their weapon of choice, making them vulnerable to detection at each step of the way."[2] In addition, "a surprisingly large number of would-be attackers either reach out to other people for help conducting the attack first, or broadcast their intent to third parties through direct threats, boasts, warnings or other statements."[3]

In July of 2010, the MTA granted a license to the Department of Homeland Security (DHS) to use the *See Something, Say Something* slogan, and in 2010 DHS launched a campaign in conjunction with the Nationwide Suspicious Activity Reporting (SAR) Initiative (NSI).[4] This chapter describes the major features of this program including priority audiences, desired behaviors, audience insights, marketing mix strategies and results. As you will read, it is more than a communications campaign, with inspiration that this behavior change needs more than "words."

Social Marketing Response

Purpose & Focus

Understandably, the broader *See Something, Say Something* program focuses on a variety of relevant violent activities including firearms, bombs, and other explosive devices. This book's chapter will feature efforts of the program relevant to *decreasing public mass shootings* with a focus on *citizens reporting suspicious activities.* As noted in Chapter 1, there were an average of 400 mass shootings a year (2015-2019) in the U.S., more than one a day.[5]

Given that gun violence appears throughout our communities, from the beginning the program created partners to help extend its reach including additional federal agencies, state and local governments, transit stations, major sports leagues, entertainment venues, private businesses, places of worship and other types of organizations such as nonprofits (e.g., summer camps). Of special note is the collaboration with each of the U.S. states and territories to establish its preferred venue and process for citizen reporting of suspicious activities. In social marketing terms, this became their Product to be promoted.

Priority Audiences & Desired Behaviors

The *See Something, Say Something* program prioritizes influencing *citizens who witness suspicious activities to then report them to appropriate authorities.* Activities related to potential mass shootings may be noticed in a variety of settings from outdoor public spaces to indoor shopping malls, workplace facilities, schools, parking lots, household dwellings, and social media postings.

It is noted that this DHS program also seeks to engage *community agencies and organizations in becoming program partners* to increase visibility of the program and access to local reporting venues.

What is Suspicious Activity Relative to a Potential Public Shooting?

Given the focus of this book on reducing deaths and injuries from guns, three relevant signs of suspicious activity among the broader 15 that are noted in the See/Say materials include:

- *Expressed Or Implied Threat* (e.g., a message from a friend sharing an intent to conduct a mass shooting)
- *Observation/Surveillance* (e.g., a prolonged or unusual interest in facilities such as a sports arena)
- *Theft/Loss/Diversion* (e.g., a gun stolen from the home of a family member)

An example of an expressed or implied threat that could have been reported, but wasn't, occurred in April of 2023. A 25-year-old bank employee in Louisville, Kentucky, opened fire as fellow employees met for a morning meeting before the bank opened, killing five people and injuring eight others. It was determined by law enforcement after the attack that before heading to his job that morning, "the shooter wrote a note to his parents and a friend indicating that he was going to open fire in the bank."[6]

How to Report Suspicious Activities to Appropriate Authorities

Once a suspicious activity has been observed, it is to be reported to local law enforcement or a person of authority. Many states have established "tiplines" for reports of suspicious activity, with resources available online to determine the best phone number based on location. DHS includes on their website "5 Ws" to be reported:[7]

- *Who* or *What* you saw

- *When* you saw it
- *Where* it occurred
- *Why* it is suspicious

A common "sighting" is a message from a planned attacker. The article noted earlier by Stratfor Worldview summarized examples of "leakages":

> "On Dec. 5, for example, the San Diego Joint Terrorism Task Force arrested a man who posted videos of himself on social media in which he *pointed guns at pedestrians from a hotel room* and threatened to conduct a mass shooting. Upon conducting a search warrant on his home, authorities seized 15 firearms, including three illegally altered rifles ... On Dec. 13, a Saudi student at the University of New Mexico was also arrested and charged with illegally possessing a firearm after a concerned citizen told authorities that he had reportedly *made a list of people he wanted to kill* before he left the United States."[8]

An example of a report of suspicious activity is one from The New Jersey Office of Homeland Security and Preparedness Counterterrorism Watch (CTWatch) that provides details of success stories on their public website, describing incidents reported by citizens, as well as subsequent interventions with potential firearm perpetrators.[9] The following is an example of one of many reported overtime.

> In November of 2014, a phone call from a private citizen to the SAFE-NJ tipline alerted the CTWatch to a violent Facebook post from an individual in Newark, New Jersey. The post stated, "Today I am going to walk up to a cruiser and shoot a cop in the ... head ... CTWatch alerted the New Jersey State Police and the Newark Real-Time Crime Center of the post. The lead was entered into the New Jersey Suspicious Activity Reporting System, and other law enforcement agencies,

including the Newark FBI-Joint Terrorism Task Force, were notified. The individual was identified in less than an hour and subsequently arrested."[10]

Audience Insights

A 2020 working paper by a professor at MIT titled "Supporting Bystanders: See Something, Say Something is Not Enough" highlighted several reasons why bystanders who see something suspicious do not always take action included the following:[11]

- Distrust of investigations or the authorities that conduct them
- Fear of bad personal consequences such as loss of relationships
- Not knowing whether what they observed warrants reporting on
- Concern they may be wrong
- Not knowing when and how to respond

What is needed, the paper emphasizes, is a systems approach, one that "deals as well as possible" with each of these barriers. The following section on key strategies provides details of the DHS program elements, clearly ones to address bystanders' concerns including not knowing what activities are suspicious enough to report, and when and how to report them to a "safe place."

Key Strategies

Campaign Materials, Messages and Communication Channels for Partners to Utilize

Although over the years *campaign materials* have evolved, as of 2023 the core message *"If You See Something, Say Something.®"* has not changed. DHS makes available general resources, as well as a bundle of materials customized for specific states and jurisdictions including posters, social media graphics, public service announcements, infographics, and pocket cards. Importantly, given this community-based approach, materials are translated in 12+ languages.[12]

Key *messages* on materials are consistent and support the two major desired actions:[13]

- **Recognize the Signs:** 15 distinct warning signs of suspicious activity are highlighted in campaign materials, including a description as well as a unique and representative graphic for each sign.
- **Report Suspicious Activities:** Campaign materials stress options for reporting suspicious activity including local law enforcement, a person of authority, and/or your state's designated "tipline." Partners are encouraged, however, to determine a singular reporting mechanism so that citizens see consistent messaging on where to report suspicious activity, helping to ensure reports are received, analyzed, and shared by designated law enforcement officials.

Partners are encouraged to use a variety of *communication channels* including social media, websites, billboards, transportation hubs, transit shuttles, parking lots, news channels for public service announcements, and on site at local businesses and event venues. Given the incidence of workplace shootings, partners are encouraged to place materials throughout office spaces, and to conduct orientations to train employees on how to recognize the signs of potential firearm violence.

Product, Price and Place Strategies for Partners and Citizens

More than a communications campaign, this DHS program also provides partners and citizens with *products, incentives,* and *convenience of access:*

- Suspicious Activity Reporting (SAR) *numbers* are identified by each state's homeland security advisor, with required features including being monitored by an individual 24 hours a day, 365 days a year . Numbers appear on campaign materials as the best number for reporting suspicious activity, which may be to call 9-1-1, or it may be a unique toll-free number identified as one to use to report suspicious activity. In addition, an interactive map on a DHS website provides each state's designated number.

- DHS provides services for partners such as *graphic design support* for localized materials, and *ready-to-print electronic files* of replicable DHS materials.

- Although downloadable materials may be used at no cost (*incentives*), partnering organizations are responsible for production (*cost*) and distribution of the materials (*place*).

- A great example of recognition (*nonmonetary incentive*) is one practice mentioned earlier in the chapter adopted by the State of New Jersey's Office of Homeland Security and Preparedness. On their website they feature success stories over the years of suspicious activity reporting by citizens. For each story, they describe in a few sentences the incident that occurred, what was reported on, and outcomes of the intervention, such as the number of lives saved.[14]

Results

Several indicators of campaign diffusion across the U.S. include:

- All U.S. states and territories have a designated number to **Report Suspicious Activity**, with 9-1-1 being the number for many states.

- In 2018, DHS declared September 25 as the National *#SeeSayDay*, a day every year in the future when DHS and its campaign partners across the country will come together to remind the public to recognize suspicious activity and how to report it to law enforcement.[15]

- As of 2023, the program has 250+ official campaign partners that span across multiple industries to include law enforcement, state and local governments, sports and entertainment, hospitality, transit, academia, not-for-profit organizations, and private companies. There are also additional organizations who proactively leverage free online DHS materials to raise awareness in their communities.[16]

Applicable Behavior Change Theories

Creating a Social Norm:[17] Increasing the reach and frequency of the campaign slogan and materials through a variety of partners in communities is an approach that can strengthen perceptions that reporting is a norm. This then can lessen perceived barriers to "saying something" including potential distrust of investigations or the authorities that conduct them, fear of bad personal consequences such as loss of relationships, and not knowing whether what they observed warrants reporting on.

Increasing Perceptions of Self-Efficacy:[18] The consistent use in materials of labels and graphics depicting clear suspicious activities addresses one of the major barriers to action, that of knowing whether or not something noticed is suspicious. In addition, clear instructions are provided on numbers to use for reporting, and the 5Ws to be prepared to report on.

Addressing Stages of Change:[19] As noted, program developers are clear this is a two-step process, with the first being the need to know the signs of suspicious activities, and the second to report on it. Unique program elements including messages and graphics address each of these stages.

Social Marketing Principles Contributing to Success[20]

Social Marketing principles included in this case example include:

Highlight Diversity, Equity, and Inclusion Best Practices: The DHS Campaign Information Packet emphasizes that factors such as race, ethnicity, gender national origin, religion, sexual orientation, and gender identity are "not suspicious."[21] It is elaborated in campaign materials for partners that the campaign is focused on the public reporting only suspicious *behaviors, rather than someone's appearance.*

Use Communication Channels at the Point of Decision-Making: Based in part on where these occur major channels include subways (see Figure 17.1), transit centers, retail shopping malls, sports arenas, entertainment venues, parking garages, and workplace cafeterias.

17.1 *An example of a communication channel at the point of decision making*

Source: Steven Lek, CC BY-SA 4.0 https://creativecommons.org/licenses /by-sa/4.0, via Wikimedia Commons

References

1 U.S. Department of Homeland Security, "If you see something, say something: Campaign Information Packet" (2018-Present), accessed at https://www. dhs.gov/sites/default/files/2022-09/S4_Campaign%20Information%20 Packet%202022.pdf

2 The National Interest, "How Well Does "See Something, Say Something" Work to Stop Terrorism?" (January 2020), accessed at https://national interest.org/blog/buzz/how-well-does-see-something-say-something-work-stop-terrorism-114586

3 Ibid.

4 U.S. Department of Homeland Security, "If you see something, say something: Campaign Information Packet" (2018-Present), accessed at https://www. dhs.gov/sites/default/files/2022-09/S4_Campaign%20Information%20 Packet%202022.pdf

5 Gun Violence Archive, "Gun Violence Archive 2023, Evidence Based Research – Since 2013" (July 2023), accessed at https://www.gunviolencearchive.org/

6 CNN, "What we know about the gunman who opened fire at a Louisville bank" (April 2023), accessed at https://www.cnn.com/2023/04/10/us/ connor-sturgeon-louisville-bank-mass-shooting/index.html

7 Department of Homeland Security, "How to Report Suspicious Activity" (June 2023) , accessed at https://www.dhs.gov/see-something-say-something /how-to-report-suspicious-activity

8 The National Interest, "How Well Does "See Something, Say Something" Work to Stop Terrorism?" (January 2020), accessed at https://national interest.org/blog/buzz/how-well-does-see-something-say-something-work-stop-terrorism-114586

9 State of New Jersey, Office of Homeland Security and Preparedness, "NJSARS Success Stories" (2006-2023), accessed at https://www.njohsp.gov/njsars-success-stories

10 Ibid.

11 MIT Sloan Working Paper, "Supporting Bystanders: See Something, Say Something is Not Enough" (2020), Prof. M. Rowe, accessed at https:// mitsloan.mit.edu/shared/ods/documents?PublicationDocumentID=8121

12 U.S. Department of Homeland Security, "If you see something, say something: Campaign Information Packet" (2018-Present), accessed at

https://www.dhs.gov/sites/default/files/2022-09/S4_Campaign%20
Information%20Packet%202022.pdf

[13] Ibid.

[14] State of New Jersey, Office of Homeland Security and Preparedness, "NJSARS Success Stories" (2006-2023), accessed at https://www.njoh sp.gov/njsars-success-stories

[15] U.S. Department of Homeland Security, "If you see something, say something: Campaign Information Packet" (2018-Present), accessed at https://www.dhs.gov/sites/default/files/2022-09/S4_Campaign%20Infor mation%20Packet%202022.pdf

[16] Personal communication from N. Ketudat, June 19, 2023.

[17] N. Lee, P. Kotler, and J. Colehour, *Social Marketing: Behavior Change for Good,* 7th Ed. (Thousand Oaks, CA: SAGE, 2024), pp. 84-86.

[18] N. Lee, P. Kotler, and J. Colehour, *Social Marketing: Behavior Change for Good,* 7th Ed. (Thousand Oaks, CA: SAGE, 2024), p.83.

[19] N. Lee, P. Kotler, and J. Colehour, *Social Marketing: Behavior Change for Good,* 7th Ed. (Thousand Oaks, CA: SAGE, 2024), pp. 78-79.

[20] N. Lee, P. Kotler, and J. Colehour, *Social Marketing: Behavior Change for Good,* 7th Ed. (Thousand Oaks, CA: SAGE, 2024)

[21] U.S. Department of Homeland Security, "If you see something, say something: Campaign Information Packet" (2018-Present) p.2, accessed at https://www.dhs.gov/sites/default/files/2022-09/S4_Campaign%20Infor mation%20Packet%202022.pdf

Chapter 18

Social Media Groups
Mitigating Potential Gun Violence

Background

Some may be surprised, even taken aback, by the topic for this chapter, with concerns that social media has downsides and has actually contributed to gun violence. An article published by the Warren Alpert Medical School at Brown University elaborates on this possibility: "Studies have suggested that social media has contributed to the rise and proliferation of gun violence across the county encouraging imitative behaviors, provoking retaliative actions, and offering bragging rights in some online communities. In addition, social media has made private information such as real-time locations, personal violent imagery and discourse, and gang threats and affiliation easily accessible to the public?"[1] The article goes on to state, however, that: "Despite these negative connotations, technology and social media have the power to reverse these trends and develop productive solutions."[2] This chapter highlights the "upside" of this messenger strategy and communication channel, leveraging its visibility, appeal, and social networks to influence "behaviors for good."

As noted in several other chapters, including Chapter 1: *The Facts*, social media postings can provide warning signs for planned gun violence homicides, mass shootings, and suicides:

- *"78% of school shooters revealed their plans ahead of time, often on social media."*[3] For example, the 18-year-old who killed 19 students and two teachers at Robb Elementary School in Uvalde, Texas, posted a photo of two AR15-style rifles on Instagram three days before going to the school.[4]

- A finding that appeared in a *SAGE* Publications journal article on "How Mass Public Shooters Use Social Media" emphasized that: "Data shows a large number of mass shooters posted some kind of indication of their thinking on the internet prior to shooting and some spelled out their violent intentions explicitly ... At the same time, the data show law enforcement has missed opportunities to prevent violence by not taking seriously past social media missives that promised violence."[5] An example included in the article described a social media posting by a mass shooter, prior to his shooting and killing nine people at an Oregon Community College. His posting was about a gunman who, 5 days prior, had killed two television journalists. "On an interesting note, I have noticed that so many people like him are alone and unknown, yet when they spill a little blood, the whole world knows who they are. A man who was known by on one, is now known by everyone. His face splashed across every screen, his name across the lips of every person on the planet all in the course of one day. Seems the more people you kill, the more you're in the limelight."[6]

- Relative to suicides and social media, an article published on *healthline* included a quote from a co-founder of *Suicide Prevention and Social Media* that "the anonymity and distance afforded by the internet can sometimes make people more likely to open up about things they'd have a harder time speaking about face to face."[7]

This chapter will highlight interventions inspired by these statistics that social media is a resource to consider for identifying, and intervening with, potential acts of gun violence.

A Social Marketing Approach

Purpose & Focus

The social marketing approach presented in this chapter features efforts to *reduce gun deaths and injuries* with a focus on *responding to social media warning signs*.

According to the *Wikipedia Encyclopedia*: "Social media are interactive technologies that facilitate the creation and sharing of information, ideas, interests, and other forms of expression through virtual communities and networks ... and it is estimated that, in 2022, there are around 3.96 billion people who are using social media around the globe."[8] Popular social media networks include Twitter, Facebook, YouTube, Instagram, Snapchat, TikTok, Reddit and LinkedIn; and some of the primary "draws" for individuals is as a news source, a social tool, a self-presentation tool, and as a health behavior change and reinforcement tool.[9] Relative to positive health-related behavior change, is has been noted that social media can be a supportive system for mental health, obesity, addiction, immunizations and more. And relative to the topic for this chapter, social media "has become perceived as a trustworthy source of information", and that "the continuous interpersonal connectivity on social media may lead to users regarding peer recommendations as indicators of the reliability of information sources."[10]

Priority Audience & Desired Behaviors

This intervention strategy prioritizes those who are *members of, and engage frequently in, one or more social media* platforms. The intended behavior is twofold. The first step is to *recognize a posting on social media that is a high risk warning sign of potential gun violence* by a family member, friend, community acquaintance, business colleague, or a fellow member of a social media group. The second action is to then *respond to this posting* in a way that mitigates a potential violent act. Potential response venues include:

- Sending a private message to the person who created the post
- Sending a private message to a third party that may be of help
- Contacting the social media platform used for the posting
- Connecting one-on-one in some other way with the person posting the message, such as via a phone call or in person visit

Audience Insights

Potential perceived barriers, desired benefits, and motivators for each of the desired behaviors are outlined in Tables 18.1 and 18.2.

Barriers	Benefits	Motivators
Not knowing if the post is a high risk one, or even a warning, for potential gun violence	Believing this could prevent potential gun deaths	Having clear guidelines for recognizing a post as one that is indicative of "high risk" for gun violence

Table 18.1: *Recognizing a High Risk Posting: Potential Barriers, Benefits, Motivators*

Barriers	Benefits	Motivators
Not knowing: • Who to respond to or notify • What to say in the response • What not to say	Saving the life of a family member or friend Saving potential victims, in addition to the potential shooter	Clear instructions/guidelines on: • What to say in a response that will help • What not to say in a response • Who to respond to • Best way to contact/follow up
Concern my response could lead to: • Retaliation against me • Increased likelihood they will carry it out • Amplifying something such as urban violence	Could deter and/or de-escalate an event Could mitigate conflicts	Data confirming this can be less dangerous than in person Confidence that this is something I can do right Brief and customized trainings

Table 18.2: *Responding to a High Risk Posting: Potential Barriers, Benefits, Motivators*

Key Strategies

Questions potential responders have regarding strategies are often related to when to respond, what to say, what not to say, and whether there are others they should reach out to. As referenced below, several of these insights and recommendations appeared in an article in the *Journal of Community Psychology*, as well as a few others.[11]

Potential *signs of risk* in the content of the post include:

- Threats of violence to other individuals or communities (e.g., a threat to beat up someone)[12]
- Content suggesting imminent gang activity (e.g., posts with pictures of gang symbols)[13]
- Postings suggesting an intent to harm (e.g., A message the Nashville school shooter in 2023 posted to a friend on Instagram: "This is my last goodbye." "You will soon be reading about it on the news after I die." "One day this will make more sense."[14])
- Expressing wanting to die (e.g., "I wish I weren't alive.")
- Words indicating emotional distress (e.g., sadness, anger, loneliness, grief) [15]

Tips from a variety of sources for *messages* include a few "dos and don'ts":

- Show empathy (e.g., "I understand you are angry about what they said to you. I would be too.")
- Don't deny/make wrong their comments (e.g., "Oh, there's nothing wrong with you, just buck up."[16])
- Suggest someone they might talk to for help (e.g., a school counselor or human resource manager)
- Offer to get together (e.g., "How about I come over?")
- In cases of threats of community violence, a police department could post a warning on a social media platform such as Twitter (e.g., "We are responding to the report of a shooter at Brown Library at First and Main Streets . . If you are inside Brown Library, shelter in place."[17])

Consider *reaching out to others close to the person* such as a family member or friend, and sharing what you noticed and asking for their advice and help.

It is also an option to reach out for *help from social media platforms*, with the following examples of procedures for two platforms noted by Nationwide Children's Hospital:

- For *Facebook*, there is an online form to submit the name of the person and the link to their Facebook profile and content of a posting of concern. A trained member of the Facebook's Community Operations Team will review the post and provide feedback regarding whether the person is at risk and will share options for support.[18]
- *Instagram* offers a different approach, providing an opportunity to request that Instagram sends the person of concern a message such as: "Someone saw one of your posts and thinks you might be having a difficult time. If you need support, we'd like to help."[19] Potential resources are then suggested and shared. The person alerting Instagram remains anonymous.

Examples

With a special interest in mitigating urban violence, Professors Forrest Stuart at Stanford University, and Jeffrey Lane at Rutgers University, concluded from data drawn from a ten year field study in Harlem and Chicago's South Side, between 2009 and 2019, that:[20]

- Social media offers an historic level of *community visibility*.
- Third parties can serve as a *vital protective* factor against violence.

In an article published in *Qualitative Sociology* in 2022, Stuart and Lane shared two examples of social media mitigating potential urban violence, both involving neighborhood third parties:

A Street Pastor: In Harlem, a man known as Pastor, seen as a key community outreach figure with more than a thousand

Twitter connections in the community, used the visibility of potential conflicts on Twitter to warn and mobilize parents and other neighborhood adults as to locations where a fight or shooting seemed imminent. He also sometimes persuaded adults to "take action when he felt like they were not doing enough."[21] One example was after two fights among large groups of girls, Pastor texted that "Word on the street they will be at it again. Won't be long before the guys get involved. I wonder what parents are waiting for ... If we don't get involved to end this, the second wave is coming."[22]

A Sister Protector: On Chicago's South Side, a 15 year old sister was concerned about her younger brother. He had connected with a local gang faction, and she was fearful that his online behavior could draw aggression from nearby gang rivals. When she noticed he had posted photos on his social media profile with a woman she had seen on profiles of young men associated with a rival gang, she was concerned. She shared with him that she had seen this woman's photo on the sites of several young men, though she didn't mention they were men belonging to rival gangs, fearful that this might insight him to challenge his rivals. "Discouraged by the thought of the young woman's multiple sexual partners, he severed ties with the woman."[23]

Applicable Behavior Change Theories

This chapter's focus on social media as a strategy certainly leverages the *Self-Perception Theory*[24] which suggests that the more we engage people in a behavior category, in this case social media engagement, the greater the chances they will sustain the activity, even take on more. Responders who begin monitoring for potential gun violence warning signs, and then respond to them, will likely continue to "be on the lookout."

It is also noted that the *Behavioral Economics Framework*[25], one that looks at how environmental and other factors prompt personal actions, backs up the appropriateness of acknowledging and responding to personal behaviors (and decisions) even though they may not be rational. Guidelines for responders that were noted in the chapter included recommendations for empathy, versus "making wrong."

Social Marketing Principles Contributing to Success[26]

Social marketing principles supportive of this case include:

- *Consider using a social media channel,* especially when priority audiences are frequent users and when messengers are needed that will be seen as trustworthy and credible.
- The need to focus on *single, simple, doable behaviors, one at a time* was adhered to in this case, with barriers, benefits and motivators identified separately for each of the two desired behaviors, first noticing postings that may be high risk warning signs, and then responding and/or reaching out.
- Providing potential responders with an option to "simply" respond directly to the post or refer the person with the concerning post to a resource for support, is certainly an example of *making access easy.*

References

[1] The Warren Alpert Medical School, "How Technology Can Combat the Increasing Gun Violence" A. Baktha, (July 2022), accessed at https://digitalhealth.med.brown.edu/news/2022-07-29/reducing-gun-violence

[2] Ibid.

[3] The Conversation, "School shooters usually show these signs of distress long before they open fire, our database shows" (February 2019), accessed at https://theconversation.com/school-shooters-usually-show-these-signs-of-distress-long-before-they-open-fire-our-database-shows-111242

[4] CNN, "Gunman posted images of guns just days ago on social media" (n.d.), accessed at Video: Texas shooter posted images of guns just days ago on social media I CNN

[5] SAGE Journals, "How Mass Public Shooters Use Social Media: Exploring Themes and Future Directions", J. Peterson et al., (February 2023) p.12, accessed at https://journals.sagepub.com/doi/10.1177/20563051231155101

[6] Ibid., p.2.

[7] Healthline, "What to Do If You See Someone Posting Thoughts of Suicide Online", L. Campbell (May 2019), accessed at https://www.healthline.com/health-news/what-to-do-when-you-encounter-suicidal-posts-online#How-best-to-respond-to-suicidal-posts-online

[8] WIKIPEDIA, "Social media", (April 2023), accessed at https://en.wikipedia.org/wiki/Social_media

[9] Ibid.

[10] Ibid.

[11] Sichel CE, Javdani S., Shaw S, Liggett R. A role for social media: A community-based response to guns, gangs, and violence online. *J Community Psychology. 2021;49:822-837.* https://doi.org/10.1002/jcop.22369

[12] Ibid.

[13] Ibid.

[14] The Independent, "Nashville school shooter's chilling final messages to a friend revealed: 'Something bad is about to happen' (March 2023), accessed at https://www.msn.com/en-us/news/crime/nashville-school-shooter-s-chilling-final-messages-to-friend-revealed-something-bad-is-about-to-happen/ar-AA19akw4

15 Sichel CE, Javdani S., Shaw S, Liggett R. "A role for social media? A community-based response to guns, gangs, and violence online." *J Community Psychology. 2021;49:822-837.* https://doi.org/10.1002/jcop.22369

16 Healthline, "What to Do If You See Someone Posting Thoughts of Suicide Online", L. Campbell (May 2019), accessed at https://www.healthline.com/health-news/what-to-do-when-you-encounter-suicidal-posts-online#How-best-to-respond-to-suicidal-posts-online

17 POLICE1, J. Parker, "4 things Law Enforcement should do on social media during an active shooter incident" (November 2018), accessed at https://julieparkercommunications.com/4-things-law-enforcement-should-do-on-social-media-during-an-active-shooter-incident/

18 NATIONWIDE CHILDREN'S, "Warning Signs of Suicide on Social Media: What You Cn Do When It's Someone You Know", (March 2019), accessed at https://www.nationwidechildrens.org/family-resources-education/700 childrens/2019/03/warning-signs-of-suicide-on-social-media

19 Ibid.

20 Lane J., Stuart F., *Qualitative Sociology*, "How Social Media Use Mitigates Urban Violence: Communication Visibility and Third-Party Intervention Processes in Digital Urban Contexts" (August 2022), accessed at https://doi.org/10.1007/s11133-022-09510-w

21 Ibid.

22 Ibid.

23 Ibid.

24 N. Lee, P. Kotler, and J. Colehour, *Social Marketing: Behavior Change for Good,* 7th Ed. (Thousand Oaks, CA: SAGE, 2024), p.80.

25 N. Lee, P. Kotler, and J. Colehour, *Social Marketing: Behavior Change for Good,* 7th Ed. (Thousand Oaks, CA: SAGE, 2024), pp.86-87.

26 N. Lee, P. Kotler, and J. Colehour, *Social Marketing: Behavior Change for Good,* 7th Ed. (Thousand Oaks, CA: SAGE, 2024)

Chapter 19

Local Governmental Agencies
Distributing Free Gun Locking Devices

Background

This is a second chapter that highlights the potential for reducing gun deaths and injuries by increasing safe gun storage and the use of locking devices. Chapter 3 highlighted programs focusing on influencing gunowners with youth/children in their home to reduce gun suicides by storing guns safely. This chapter focuses on a broader community-based approach, one with an intention to decrease access to guns among unauthorized users/criminals, as well as raising public support for this practice. Data regarding the involvement of stolen guns in deaths and injuries confirm the need for this chapter's focus:

- Some studies have estimated that more than 80% of those arrested for a gun crime were armed with a stolen gun.[1]
- Almost half of school shooters stole the gun from a family member.[2]
- Between 200,000 and 500,000 guns are stolen from individuals every year.[3]
- Nearly one fourth of stolen guns are taken from cars and other vehicles.[4]
- Stolen guns often end up in the possession of someone who is legally prohibited from having a gun.[5]
- Between 2006 and 2016, the number of guns reported stolen from individuals increased by nearly 60%.[6]

A study at the University of Washington conducted by Ali Rowhani-Rahbar, Joseph Simonetti and Frederick Rivara included a systematic review of available research to determine the efficacy of a variety of interventions to influence the *use of gun lock devices*. Three intervention program results were compared. One program provided two "products", *free securing devices as well as counseling on the importance of securing guns*; a second study group program provided *counseling only*; and a third was a *control group*. Findings were inspiring and informative:[7]

- Among the two groups who received a free gun securing device as well as counseling, only **35 percent reported now having unlocked guns in their homes.**
- Among those in the control group, **89 percent reported having unlocked guns in their homes.**
- Among the groups who received just counseling, only one showed a significant improvement in storage practices.

In summary, researchers reported that "Participants were much more likely to comply when provided with a free device to secure their firearms."[8]

This chapter highlights efforts of local governmental agencies across the U.S. who have used this proven strategy of employing a community-based program that distributes free gun locking devices.

A Social Marketing Approach Examples

Community-led initiatives designed to influence the *use of gun locking devices when firearms are not in use* (focus) are intended to *prevent theft and misuse of firearms* (purpose). Programs are most often present in communities with both a high number of gun owners, as well as a diverse group of local organizations committed to community safety. These locally designed programs are tailored to fit the unique profile of gunowners and citizens in the community, and are often in response to recent local tragic shootings.

Interestingly, one of the supporters of this approach to reducing gun deaths and injuries is NSSF, The Firearm Industry Trade Association that promotes safe gun storage and safety locks as a best practice. In 2017, their Industry Intelligence Report confirmed the "acceptance" of gun locks as a secure storage method, reporting that 32% of gun owners were currently using gun locks.[9] The report also noted that one program promoted by NSSF, Project ChildSafe, is seen as a best practice, highlighting that through this program "more than 37 million gun locks have been distributed – free of charge – to more than 15,000 communities in every state and U.S. territory."[10] And in 2018, Project ChildSafe supported and promoted the world's first biometric fingerprint trigger lock for fireams.[11]

The following seven examples of community-based programs with a focus on distributing free gun locks include several supported by NSSF. As you will read, strategies are aligned with overcoming barriers to safe storage by offering monetary incentives; providing easy access to devices; increasing perceived norms for safe storage among community members, as well as by the firearm industry; and highlighting the desired benefit of saving lives.

Minnesota's Public Event Strategy: As stated on their website "Make Minnesota Safe & Secure", the State of Minnesota has an ambitious goal to "get a gun lock into the hands of every Minnesota gun owner who doesn't already have one."[12] A news release in 2022 promoted a free gun lock giveaway program at the state's annual Minnesota State Fair, stating that: "Stopping by our booth and picking up a gun lock costs nothing. But saving even one life is priceless."[13] It was further reported that "The program, which is part of a $1 million investment in gun safety paid for with federal

American Rescue funds, includes the departments of public safety, health, agriculture, natural resources, veterans affairs and other state agencies."[14] A follow up story on their website in 2023 mentions that more than *50,00 gun locks have been given away since 2022,* and if haven't gotten one they can fill out an online request form, or visit a department nearby to pick one up.[15]

Philadelphia, Pennsylvania, Featuring a Credible Messenger: In 2022, Philadelphia's Sheriff Rochelle Bilal was featured at a conference, and in a follow up video on the city's website, strongly requesting that "If you *Got a Gun? Get a Lock!"*[16] The Sheriff's office, in partnership with the City Council, expressed their commitment to distributing free gun locks to promote safe firearm containment practices that help prevent theft and misuse. Comments in the video and on the website "shout out" that citizens can either pick one up at the front desk of the Sheriff's Office, Monday-Friday between 8:30am and 4:30pm, or can call a hotline number for more information. In addition, promotional materials provide instructive information to assure gun owners that "Using a gun lock is easy." The *Got a Gun? Get a Lock*! program is also promoted at the annual traditional National Night Out special event where free gun locks and how-to information are distributed.[17]

St. Louis, Missouri, Using a Timely Reminder Strategy: On March 30, 2022, it was announced that after several tragic shootings were reported in the past week alone, St. Louis City leaders were urging residents (once more) to access the city's free *Lock It For Love* gun lock program. Locks can be picked up at one of 30 fire engine stations open 24 hours a day, at specific library branches, and at police departments. The announcement also included access to a video tutorial on how to use a gunlock on a firearm, available on YouTube.[18] A quote from the city's Mayor reinforced the urgent need. "If you have a gun in the house, be a responsible gun owner; store firearms locked and unloaded and pick up a free gun lock to help you and your loved ones be safe."[19] As of March 2022, the *Lock It for Love* program had *distributed 8,000 gun locks.*[20]

Project ChildSafe: Supporting Lock Promotions and Distributions by Community Groups[21]

As noted, several of this chapter's program examples of community-led initiatives are supported by Project ChildSafe, a program initially launched as a Department of Justice Bureau of Justice Assistance grant program. In partnership with local community organizations, activities focus on providing free cable-style gun locks for distribution to local citizens, and gun safety education to firearm owners, as well as to non-gun owners. Strategies underscore the importance of securing firearms when not in use. Programs are tailored to best fit the needs of the community, with an emphasis on authentic communications and trusted messengers. Community partners are diverse, often including law enforcement agencies, community centers, faith groups, local governments, suicide prevention advocates, veterans' organizations, retailers, conservation groups, and hunting and shooting groups. Project ChildSafe's website includes information and links for local law enforcement agencies to register as a law enforcement partner and receive free safety devices to be distributed in their community.[22]

Two programs featured next are ones that were part of Project ChildSafe's initial successful pilot program in 2017, with a $2.4 million Department of Justice grant providing free gun locks, as well as media relations support. Since the end of the program in 2019, these communities continue to sustain momentum through a coalition of supporters.

Oklahoma City, Oklahoma, Partnering with Law Enforcement Agencies and News Outlets:[23] The main lock distribution partners in the Oklahoma City community are the City's Police Department,

Fire Department, and the County Sheriff's Office. One inspiring strategy is the partnership the community stakeholders formed with a local broadcast station KFOR. In addition to paid media buys, KFOR donated more than 46 hours of airtime, supporting visibility for the program and a PSA titled *Safety Is a Habit* which demonstrates the simple procedure for inserting the trigger lock. Visibility was also increased through social media spreading firearm safety messages, as well as through a region-wide student essay contest. As of 2019, this pilot project that was launched in 2017 had distributed nearly 11,000 gun locks and safety materials to local residents.[24] And as of 2022, Project ChildSafe continues to supply free gunlocks for distribution to the Oklahoma City community.

Memphis, Tennessee, Increasing Distribution Channels:[25] When this pilot project launched in 2017, a city-wide lock distribution event included six location across the metro area, distributing 2,500 locks. Since this launch additional distribution locations have been enhanced, with community centers and faith based organizations not only providing convenient locations for pickup, but also delivering frequent communications reminding gunowners how vital gun safety is "to keeping loved ones safe." Similar to the program in Oklahoma City, a partnership was formed with a local broadcast station WATN, which aired the Safety Is a Habit PSA. It was published in 2018 that more than *19,700 free gun locks have been distributed* to the Memphis community.[26]

Applicable Behavior Change Theories

Perhaps the strongest behavior change theory represented by these programs are efforts to create a *perceived public norm*[27] for gunowners to use locking devices. Building this norm is accomplished by a variety of tactics including booths at highly visible public events such as the Minnesota State Fair, messages and messengers from numerous and diverse governmental agencies, and participation of local community organizations in the distribution of free locking devices including public libraries, community centers and faith-based organizations.

Social Marketing Principles Contributing to Success[28]

One of the major social marketing principles contributing to this case example's success is that of *using important criteria to select a desired behavior*. For this program, the desired behavior for gunowners to use a gun locking device was seen as one that would reduce gun deaths and injuries by decreasing firearm access for unauthorized users. Based on Doug McKenzie-Mohr's framework, it meets one of the five important criteria for behavior selection, that of potential *Impact*. Impact is determined by affirming that if your audience adopts the behavior, it will "make a difference relative to the purpose of your campaign."[29] Program planners should also ask the question, "How does this compare with other potential behaviors?"

With a focus on reducing unauthorized use of guns, another potential behavior that might be considered is that of *taking an unwanted or unused gun to a local law enforcement office*. Programs with this focus have been implemented in many states across the U.S., and are known as Gun Buy Back programs, and include some form of monetary incentive in exchange for the gun such as a gift card or cash. Several research studies, including one from Harvard Kennedy School titled "Gun buybacks: What the research says", question whether the program will actually result in reducing firearm deaths (impact). [30] Even though many gunowners show up at special events and sheriff departments to "give up" their gun (outcome), does this actually reduce access to functioning guns among unauthorized users? Several studies note concerns regarding the condition of the guns that are turned in at these events. "Most gun buyback initiatives turn up old or broken weapons - and cost police departments thousands of dollars in the process."[31] In addition, gunowners turning in the gun for an incentive may still have other guns in their home, or use the incentive to buy another one. In the end, there is mixed evidence as to whether gun buyback programs, versus distribution of free gun locking devices, have significant impact in reducing access to guns that would be used for violent crime by unauthorized users.

Another principle contributing to success of these programs is the variety of tools in the toolbox that are being used to influence using a gun locking device:

- **Product**: Locking devices, such as a cable or fingerprint trigger lock, and instructional materials that demonstrate how it can be easily installed
- **Price**: Free lock giveaways, and partners acknowledging those receiving a free lock for doing the right thing (nonmonetary incentive)
- **Place**: Providing multiple local outlets to access a free lock including at popular community events, local police and fire stations, community centers and faith-based organizations
- **Promotion**: Featuring credible messengers, airing public service announcements, highlighting the benefit of saving lives, and memorable slogans such as *Got a Gun? Get a Lock*, and *Lock It For Love*

References

[1] Bev Fitchett's Guns, " What Percentage of Crimes Are Committed With Stolen Guns?" (June 2023), accessed at https://www.bevfitchett.us/gun-laws/what-percentage-of-crimes-are-committed-with-stolen-guns.html

[2] BROOKINGS, "School shootings: What we know about them, and what we can do to prevent them" (January 2022), R. Kowalski, accessed at https://www.brookings.edu/blog/brown-center-chalkboard/2022/01/26/school-shootings-what-we-know-about-them-and-what-we-can-do-to-prevent-them/

[3] EVERYTOWN, "Stolen Guns Pose a Tremendous Risk to Public Safety" (March 2019), accessed at https://everytownresearch.org/report/stolen-guns-pose-a-tremendous-risk-to-public-safety/

[4] Ibid.

[5] Ibid.

[6] Ibid.

[7] THE TRACE, "Freebies May Be the Key to Success to Safe Gun Storage Programs" (March 2016), accessed at https://www.thetrace.org/2016/03/safe-gun-storage-research/

[8] Ibid.

[9] NSSF The Firearm Industry Trade Association, "The Success of Safe Storage Programs, By the Numbers" (September 2017), accessed at https://www.nssf.org/articles/the-success-of-safe-storage-programs-by-the-numbers/

[10] Ibid.

[11] IDENTILOCK, "IDENTILOCK CHOSEN AS THE GRAND PRIZE IN PROJECT CHILDSAFE'S 4TH ANNUAL FRIENDS AND FAMILY CAMPAIAGN" (May 24, 2018), accessed at https://getidentilock.com/blogs/news/identilock-grand-prize-project-childsafe

[12] Make Minnesota Safe & Secure, "Free Gun Locks" (2023), accessed at https://dps.mn.gov/safe-secure/Pages/default.aspx

[13] Minnesota Department of Public Safety, "State of Minnesota Launches Free Gun Lock Giveaway" (August 2022), accessed at https://dps.mn.gov/divisions/ooc/news-releases/Pages/state-minnesota-launches-free-gun-lock-giveaway.aspx#:~:text=%E2%80%98Make%20Minnesota%20Safe

%20%26%20Secure%E2%80%99%20Aims%20to%20Put,them%20out%20at%20their%20Minnesota%20State%20Fair%20booths.

[14] Ibid.

[15] Make Minnesota Safe & Secure, "Free Gun Locks" (2023), accessed at https://dps.mn.gov/safe-secure/Pages/default.aspx

[16] Philadelphia Sheriff Department, "Got a Gun-Get a Lock!" (2023), accessed at https://phillysheriff.com/gunprogram/

[17] Philadelphia Sheriff Department, "Office Of The Philadelphia Sheriff Continues Its Community Engagement Commitment With Residents." (August 2022), accessed at https://phillysheriff.com/commitment-with-residents/

[18] STLOUIS-MO GOV, "City of St. Louis Urges Residents to Utilize "Lock It For Love" Gun Lock Program at St. Louis Fire Engine Houses, Select Public Library Branches, Area SLMPD Stations" (March 30, 2022), accessed at https://www.stlouis-mo.gov/government/departments/mayor/news/lock-it-for-love.cfm

[19] Ibid.

[20] Ibid.

[21] PROJECT CHILDSAFE, "Focus Communities" (2019), accessed at https://projectchildsafe.org/focus-communities/

[22] PROJECT CHILDSAFE, "LAW ENFORCEMENT" (2018), accessed at https://projectchildsafe.org/law-enforcement/

[23] PROJECT CHILDSAFE, "Focus Communities" (2019), accessed at https://projectchildsafe.org/focus-communities/

[24] Ibid.

[25] Ibid.

[26] Ibid.

[27] N. Lee, P. Kotler, and J. Colehour, *Social Marketing: Behavior Change for Good,* 7th Ed. (Thousand Oaks, CA: SAGE, 2024), pp.84-86.

[28] N. Lee, P. Kotler, and J. Colehour, *Social Marketing: Behavior Change for Good,* 7th Ed. (Thousand Oaks, CA: SAGE, 2024)

[29] N. Lee, P. Kotler, and J. Colehour, *Social Marketing: Behavior Change for Good,* 7th Ed. (Thousand Oaks, CA: SAGE, 2024), pp.154-155.

[30] HARVARD KENNEDY SCHOOL "Gun buybacks: What the research says" (October 2022), accessed at https://journalistsresource.org/health/gun-buybacks-what-the-research-says/

[31] The Trace, "Police Trade Cash for Thousands of Guns Each Year. But Experts Say It Does Little to Stem Violence" (July 2015), accessed at https://www.thetrace.org/2015/07/gun-buyback-study-effectivness/

Chapter 20

Governmental Agencies
Offering Monetary Incentives for Safe
Firearm Storage

Background

This is a third chapter that highlights the potential for reducing gun deaths and injuries by increasing safe gun storage, with Chapter 3 highlighting the impact of safe storage on *preventing youth suicide*, and Chapter 19 featuring the distribution of *free gun locking devices*. Several statistics noted throughout this book present a few clear facts warranting additional strategic options for increasing safe storage, ones worth repeating:

- Over 80% of firearm suicides by youth/children in the U.S. involve a gun belonging to a family member, relative or friend.[1]
- Almost half of school shooters stole the gun from a family member.[2]
- Some studies have estimated that more than 80% of those arrested for a gun crime were armed with a stolen gun.[3]

A Social Marketing Approach

Purpose & Focus

The social marketing approach presented in this chapter features efforts to *increase safe gun storage* with a focus on governmental agencies providing *monetary incentives.* One of the reasons this strategy features those of governmental agencies is that this approach to reducing gun deaths and injuries is often seen as one that faces fewer political hurdles. This potential is elaborated upon in an article in *The Wall Street Journal*, "Gun-Safety Incentives Draw Bipartisan Support", highlighting that "lawmakers and gun-control advocates see the issue of safe gun storage as one of the ripest areas for bipartisan consensus, as it is intended to protect children and prevent suicides without restricting the ability of gun owners to buy a firearm."[4] In addition, it is a strategy that the NRA supports, as opposed to imposing federal standards and mandates for storage. In social marketing terms, it is a "help me" behavior change approach versus a "make me" approach.

Priority Audience & Desired Behavior

Strategies highlight the use and appeal of monetary incentives to influence *gun owners,* especially those with children in the home, to *purchase safe firearm storage devices.*

Audience Insights

Insights inspiring strategies are summarized in Table 20.1.

Audience	Barriers	Benefits	Motivators
Gun owners purchasing safe storage devices	• Don't see it as necessary • Costs can be high, like for some gun safes, thousands of dollars • Storage decreases quick access to firearms when needed	• Saving lives by keeping guns from my children as well as burglars • Avoiding penalties if my gun was stolen and used for violent crime	• Monetary incentives • Options that still ensure quick access to firearms

Table 20.1 *Audience Insights for Safe Firearm Storage: Potential Barriers, Benefits, Motivators*

Key Strategies

Monetary incentives are an "attachment" of the Price "P" tool. As in commercial marketing, this tactic can be motivating, inspiring desired actions. A variety of monetary incentives offered by governmental agencies, and one nongovernmental agency, to increase purchasing of storage devices include:

Tax Credits: A tax credit for purchasing a gun safe or safety device is typically made available by the passage of a bill by state lawmakers. Restrictions may include a limit on the amount that would apply, and a requirement for receipts to be submitted when filing taxes.[5]

Rebates: Some states and local communities offer residents over the age of 21 reimbursement for the purchase of a gun safe. Common conditions include it being a one-time reimbursement and a limit of one per household. Rebate amounts are offered as a percentage of the purchase price (e.g., 25%), or it may be stated as a maximum amount (e.g., $500).[6]

Exemptions From Sales Tax: In several states, including Connecticut, Massachusetts, Michigan, New Jersey, and Washington, there are laws that exempt gun-safe purchases from a sales tax.[7] Examples of promotional headlines highlighting this monetary incentive include: "Tired of Giving Money to Uncle Sam? Gun Safes Are Tax-Free", and "Relax. There's No Tax On Gun Safes."[8]

Insurance Incentives: Benefits for nongovernmental agencies offering a monetary incentive for using safe gun storage devices was highlighted in a US Insurance Agents article on March 27, 2023, titled "Unintended Shooting are Preventable."[9] It addressed the question, "Does insurance make guns safer?" It noted that "Most unintentional shootings leading to injuries or deaths caused by firearms could have been prevented if owners properly stored their guns. Insurance companies reward good practices by *providing lower premiums,* and this incentive alone can cause more owners to adjust their gun safety."[10]

Examples of States Offering Monetary Incentives

An article on February 23, 2023, in the online *Virginia Beach Observer* described a recent enactment of a House Bill Amendment that provides a monetary incentive for safe gun storage.

> "RICHMOND, VIRGINIA — Lawmakers did not pass bills introducing penalties for improperly storing a firearm, but did agree to incentivize firearm safety through a tax credit. Lawmakers last week passed a measure introduced by Del. Alfonso Lopez, D-Arlington. The House bill, which had bipartisan support in both chambers, will create a tax credit for purchasing a firearm safety device, such as a gun safe or locker. Anyone who purchases a gun safe, or similar device that can be used to store a firearm by means of a key or combination, will be eligible for a tax credit, according to the bill. Taxable years for this credit are between Jan. 1, 2023, and Jan. 1, 2028. The purchaser of a gun safe will receive no more than one tax credit a year for up to $300 of the purchase price of one or more firearm safety devices, according to the bill. Lawmakers agreed to cap the pool of available credits allowed at $5 million annually, on a first-come, first-served basis. Taxpayers are required to submit receipts for the purchases."[11]

The website for the City of Northglenn, *Colorado,* describes their incentive for safe gun storage:

> "This program will reimburse a Northglenn resident, over the age of 21, up to 25 percent or a maximum of $500 on the purchase of an eligible gun safe. If the gun safe is purchased from a Northglenn business, the city will reimburse up to 30

percent of the cost or a maximum of $525. This program is a one-time reimbursement and is limited to one per residence ... Residents of Northglenn wishing to participate in this program may email the make and model number of the safe they wish to purchase, prior to their purchase, to make sure it meets the requirements of this program."[12]

In 1998, *Washington State* passed a law, RCW 82.08.832, which exempts the sale of gun safes from state tax. Details were also provided on the required features for the gun safe to be tax-exempt:

"The good news is — gun safes are tax-free in Washington State ... In the case of this law, the gun safe tax-exemption applies to any enclosure specifically designed or modified for the purpose of storing a firearm. The enclosure must be equipped with a padlock, key lock, combination lock, or similar locking device so that it prevents unauthorized access and use of the firearm. Gun safes equipped with electronic locks would also fall within this tax-exempt category. This means, when you shop for a gun safe in Washington, the price you see is the price you pay."[13]

Applicable Behavior Change Theories

The *Exchange Theory*[14] is front and center for this effort, given that the monetary incentive offer lowers actual costs, in some cases amounting to several hundred dollars, and the purchaser is still likely to receive the desired benefit, that of protection from harm.

This case is also an example of a framework that mirrors the *Community Based Prevention Model*[15], as a coalition of organizations are involved in the development and implementation of this monetary strategy to increase sales of safe gun storage devices, potentially including policy makers, State Departments of Revenue,

State Departments of Health, firearm retail stores, and insurance companies.

Social Marketing Principles Contributing to Success[16]

Social marketing principles supportive of this monetary incentive to increase safe gun storage include:

- *Provide incentives that will increase benefits and/or decrease costs.* Monetary incentives can take many forms, including rebates, gift cards, and price adjustments rewarding customers for adopting the desired behavior. The waiver of the sales tax and other strategies related to the purchase of safe gun storage devices not only decreased monetary costs, it also, in its "package", provides a desired benefit of protecting family members from potential harm.
- Placing promotional signs in public venues such as retail stores (e.g., The Price You See Is the Price You Pay) is in alignment with the principle of using *communication channels at the point of decision making*. In addition, this visibility certainly helps to increase the perception that safe gun storage is a *Perceived Norm*.
- As noted, the passage of laws to provide tax benefits and incentives for purchasing safe gun storage devices is seen as having fewer barriers than alternatives such as restrictions on types of guns that can be purchased, or mandatory safe storage. In other words, this policy has a *competitive advantage* for bipartisan support.
- Finally, the messages at the point of purchase that were shared (e.g., Relax. There's No Tax On Gun Safes) exude the principal of *have a little fun with messages*.

References

[1] EVERYTOWN, "Firearm Suicides in the United States" (February 2023), accessed at https://everytownresearch.org/report/firearm-suicide-in-the-united-states/

[2] BROOKINGS, "School shootings: What we know about them, and what we can do to prevent them" (January 2022), R. Kowalski, accessed at https://www.brookings.edu/blog/brown-center-chalkboard/2022/01/26/school-shootings-what-we-know-about-them-and-what-we-can-do-to-prevent-them/

[3] Bev Fitchett's Guns, " What Percentage of Crimes Are Committed With Stolen Guns?" (June 2023), accessed at https://www.bevfitchett.us/gun-laws/what-percentage-of-crimes-are-committed-with-stolen-guns.html

[4] *The Wall Street Journal*, "Gun-Safety Incentives Draw Bipartisan Support" (April 9, 2021), K. Peterson, accessed at https://www.wsj.com/articles/gun-safety-incentives-draw-bipartisan-support-11617966015

[5] The Virginia Pilot, "Virginia lawmakers pass firearm safety tax credit, kill bill requiring proper", (February 22, 2023), C. Hawkins, accessed at https://www.pilotonline.com/government/virginia/vp-nw-cns-virginia-firearms-bills-20230223-rorppn2ahfgdpm5b46elgorqgu-story.html

[6] PROTECT & LOCK, "Is a gun safe tax deductible in the United States?" (n.d.), accessed at https://www.protectandlock.com/gun-safe-tax-deductible

[7] Ibid.

[8] NW Safe, "Tired of Giving Money to Uncle Sam" Gun Safes Are Tax-Free." (February 2023), K. Johnson, accessed at https://nwsafe.com/blogs/tips/tax-free-gun-safes

[9] US Insurance, "Do you need gun liability insurance?" (March 27, 2023), L. Adams, accessed at Do you need gun liability insurance? | US Insurance Agents

[10] Ibid.

[11] Virginia Beach Observer, "Virginia lawmakers pass firearm safety tax credit, kill bill requiring proper" (February 22, 2023), E. Morin, accessed at https://thevirginiabeachobserver.com/local-news/virginia-lawmakers-pass-firearm-safety-tax-credit-kill-bill-requiring-proper-storage/

[12] Northglenn Police, "Gun Safe Program", (n.d.), accessed at https://www.northglenn.org/public_safety/police/gun_safe_program.php

[13] NW Safe, "Tired of Giving Money to Uncle Sam" Gun Safes Are Tax-Free." (February 2023), K. Johnson, accessed at https://nwsafe.com/blogs/tips/tax-free-gun-safes

[14] N. Lee, P. Kotler, and J. Colehour, *Social Marketing: Behavior Change for Good,* 7th Ed. (Thousand Oaks, CA: SAGE, 2024), p.90.

[15] Ibid., pp.90-91.

[16] N. Lee, P. Kotler, and J. Colehour, *Social Marketing: Behavior Change for Good,* 7th Ed. (Thousand Oaks, CA: SAGE, 2024).

Chapter 21

News Reporters & Journalists
Increasing Public Concern & Inspiring Action

Background

In 2020, a study published in the journal of *Preventive Medicine* examined the ways the media covers gun shootings, and commented that "the news could be painting an unrealistic picture of gun violence, which might affect the way the public perceives it."[1] Findings also supported recommendations that news reporting practices should focus on evidence-based solutions to reducing gun deaths and injuries, and that public perceptions are key to behavior change. Examples of a few news reporting practices "not reflecting reality" from this study included the following, compiled from police reports and information kept by the Gun Violence Archive group in 2017 for three different cities: Philadelphia, Cincinnati, and Rochester, NY, illustrating a disproportionate emphasis to less common circumstances and victims:[2]

- Even though 83 percent of victims of intentional shootings in these cities were Black, just 49 percent of them made the news.
- Men victims were 40 percent less likely to be covered on the news than women victims, even though they are more likely to be victims than women.
- Even though 16 percent of the victims from the analyzed shootings died, they accounted for 83 percent of the cases covered in the news, distorting the facts that a vast majority of gun violence victims are injuries and not reported on.

A similar statistic reported by ABC News pointed out that "What you don't hear about, and what people don't assess, is that for every story of a mass shooting, there are, on average, 300 other stories, most of them suicides that are never told."[3]

In the United States, there seems to be agreement that gun violence is a major public health crisis,[4] and that news reporters and journalists can and should follow public health and safety behavior change practices that can leverage the news media's visible and trusted source of information to increase public awareness, concerns, and preventive actions to help end this crisis.

A Social Marketing Approach

Purpose & Focus

The social marketing approach presented in this chapter features efforts to *increase public behaviors that can decrease gun deaths and injuries,* with a focus on *inspirational coverage by news reporters and journalists.*

Priority Audiences & Desired Behaviors

Ideally, strategies presented in this chapter will inspire news reporters and journalists for national and local news outlets to:

- Cover more *representative incidents* of gun violence circumstances and victims.
- Mention *preventive actions* citizens can take that can help reduce these incidents in the future.

Audiences for these reporters and journalists to keep in mind are those who are regular listeners of daily television and radio news programs, and readers of popular news publications. Within this segment, a priority audience are *those who could take protective actions,* as well as intervene in cases of attempted homicides and suicides. An additional priority audience for their coverage are also those most at risk for gun violence.

Audience Insights

Barriers

Concerns that reporters and journalists may have to covering gun deaths and injuries with more representative incidents and mentioning preventive actions include perspectives that:

- Covering more representative incidents of gun violence such as suicide could lead more people to end their lives that way. In other words, it has the risk of creating a "copycat effect."[5]
- Highlighting detailed information about an assailant and/or the victim could cause retaliation and put their own safety at risk.
- Emphasizing gun violence in their newscasts and journal articles could position them with some of their audiences as having "an obsession" with guns and preference for "juicy content", and not focusing enough on the "good news."
- Promoting actions that could have prevented an incident such as suicide could make some listeners feel remorse that they didn't do this.

Desired Benefits

Certainly, news reporters and journalists would be more likely to adopt these best practices if they believed this would actually *help reduce gun deaths and injuries* in their communities. In other words, the potential benefit could outweigh the risks.

Motivators

Reporters and journalists could be supported to share preventive practices by providing access to informational resources regarding facts about the gun violence landscape in terms of incidents, victims, offenders, and preventive actions. Research that helped dispel some of their major concerns, such as increasing "copy catting" and retaliation, would also be important, even necessary.

Key Strategies

Increasing Public Concern

Share persuasive facts related to gun violence in the U.S. that the public is often not aware of, ones that would increase concerns, and inspire more protective actions such as reporting on where the assailant got the gun. The following examples are ones from a variety of sources including Johns Hopkins Center for Gun Violence Solutions, Pew Research Center, and Harvard Magazine:

- On average, more than 100 Americans die every day from a gun-related injury, more than the number dying from car crashes.[6] And almost 200 more are shot and wounded a day.[7]
- The majority, more than 60%, of firearm deaths with intent each year are a result of suicides (2015 – 2019).[8]
- Gun deaths are *the leading cause of death for children and teens* since 2020.[9]
- Among children and youth under 18, over 80% of firearm suicides involve *a gun belonging to a family member.*[10]
- Nearly half of individuals engaged in mass shootings (48%) signaled their plans in advance to others, including family members, friends, and colleagues, as well as strangers and law enforcement officers.[11]

- "Notably, in 4 out of 5 school shootings, at least one other person had knowledge of the attacker's plan but failed to report it."[12]
- More than 44% of U.S. adults report living in a gun household.[13]
- About 40% of gun owners have at least one gun that is both loaded and easily accessible.[14]
- An estimated 300,000 guns are stolen each year from private owners, more than 800 a day (2020).[15]
- Some studies have estimated that more than 80 percent of those arrested for a gun crime were armed with a stolen gun.[16]
- Gun death rate in the U.S. is much higher than in most other nations, particularly among developed nations.[17] A correlated factor to firearm deaths is firearm possession, with it reported in 2017 that U.S. civilians had the *highest rate in the world of firearm possession*.[18]

Correct misinformation that may deter protective actions, illustrated by these examples:

- Some surveys have shown that most consumers think that mass shootings are the most common forms of gun violence, even though most gun deaths are suicides and interpersonal violence is second highest.[19]
- While many emphasize gun deaths in big cities like Chicago and New York, approximately half of homicides by gun occur in suburban and rural areas.[20]
- Some see arming more school officials as the best way to prevent school shootings and keep students safe, while many believe the best way to prevent gun violence at schools is to keep guns away from those intent on causing harm,[21] especially since their intent is most often known.

Highlight real stories of victims to create more credibility, empathy, and motivation to act. An article by Katherine Reed in *Neiman Reports* highlights "What Journalists Can Do To Report More Effectively – and Compassionately – On Gun Violence."[22] Recommendations noted in the article were, in part, an outcome of a Better Gun Violence Reporting Summit in Philadelphia in 2019, one exploring the most constructive ways to report on gun violence. One of those recommendations for reporters and journalists was to: "Do more stories about survivors." This approach is one substantiated by Dr. Jessica Beard, a trauma unit surgeon and lead researcher for the Philadelphia Center for Gun Violence: "Giving gun violence victims a voice in their own stories would give audiences a sense of what it looks like to survive a firearm injury, the incredible barriers people have to surmount to do that, and the incredible resilience people show."[23] It is noted that professional guidelines for interviews of victims provide more detail on when these stories may "not be a good idea", as well as recommendations for recording features, timing, and content.

Inspiring Action

Feature stories of people taking actions to help reduce gun deaths and injuries in their communities.[24] An example of this approach was an article in *The Guardian* in 2019 that featured a story about a woman living in an apartment complex in northern California who had witnessed six shootings in the past two days, and decided "to do something" to protect her neighbors.[25] As a longtime antiviolence advocate, she had experience in conducting trainings for children to recognize active shootings, and to know when and how to get to safety. Her efforts with the children in her complex began with a gathering in her home where she provided "sweet treats." Once out on the playground she gathered the kids around another big container of candy and told the kids to play on the jungle gym until they heard her yell "boom, boom, boom." When they heard it, the kids then gathered to run to a designated "safe place" near the playground. After the drill, she applauded their actions and received reassuring feedback, with comments from one child that: "It was easy. I'm just happy it wasn't a real one. Playing outside is not scary to me because I know if it happens again, I know what to do."[26]

When featuring a gun death or injury incident, mention in the news what citizens can do in the future to prevent this. A story on FOX news in 2023 featured an incident in Texas where a three-year-old girl unintentionally shot and killed her four-year-old sister. The two were inside a bedroom and family members, who heard the gunshot, ran into the bedroom and found the four-year-old girl unresponsive. She was later pronounced dead at the scene. The story ended with a message from the county sheriff stating that: "It seems like another tragic story of, again, a child gaining access to a firearm and hurting someone else, and this time it was a fatal shot, and appears to be her sibling ... It's just, again, very tragic, and very preventable. You've got to make sure you're being a responsible gun owner. Secure your weapons in a safe place."[27]

Build trusting relationships in communities most affected by gun violence.[28] This recommendation is one from the Better Gun Violence Reporting Summit, noting that these relationships can inform stories that will end up being more in depth, creating empathy, and inspiring protective actions. Potential relevant community contacts to develop relationships with include local school superintendents, police chiefs, elected officials, pastors, local service clubs, and others who are likely to have insights and potential relationships with victims, as well as offenders in their community.[29]

Applicable Behavior Change Theories

Strategies to address potential concerns that news reporters and journalists are likely to have regarding recommendations to share more representative and real stories of gun violence may be inspired by the *Social Cognitive Theory*[30] which states that likelihood of adopting the behavior will be increased if perceptions of benefits for doing this will outweigh these concerns, and that they believe they will be able to perform the behavior (self-efficacy).

Social Marketing Principles Contributing to Success[31]

Recommendations from the Philadelphia conference noted earlier certainly include several that are supportive of social marketing principles including:

- Increasing *message and messenger credibility* by telling real stories about real people
- Applying the *public health model* that emphasizes preventive behaviors and engages communities

In addition, the principle of making desired behaviors *"fun, popular, and easy"* was a strong component of the example of the "boom, boom, boom" safety drills for kids in the apartment complex.

References

[1] Penn Medicine News, "Study: Media's Reporting on Gun Violence Does Not Reflect Reality" (October 20, 2020), accessed at https://www.penn medicine.org/news/news-releases/2020/october/study-medias-reporting-on-gun-violence-does-not-reflect-reality

[2] Ibid.

[3] abcNEWS, "America has a gun violence problem. What do we do about it?" (October 25, 2021), accessed at America has a gun violence problem. What do we do about it? - ABC News (go.com)

[4] APHA, "Gun Violence Is A Public Health Crisis" (n.d.), accessed at https://www.apha.org/-/media/files/pdf/factsheets/200221_gun_violence_fact_sheet.ashx?la=en&hash=F18D18BB89294AE9EFAA2EB5C0B00B073C6 5863F

[5] The Trace, A. Tucker, "These Philadelphia Researchers Want Journalists to Tell Better Stories About gun Violence" (Feb. 23, 2023), https://www.the trace.org/2023/02/crime-news-reporting-harm-victims/

[6] Johns Hopkins Center for Gun Violence Solutions, "Quick Facts About the Public Health Approach to Prevent Gun Violence" (February 2021), accessed at https://efsgv.org/learn/learn-more-about-gun-violence/public-health-approach-to-gun-violence-prevention/

[7] Everytown for Gun Safety, "Debunking gun Myths at the Dinner Table" (October 2022), accessed at https://www.everytown.org/debunking-gun-myths-at-the-dinner-table/

[8] EFSBV, "A Public Health Crisis Decades in the Making: A Review of 2019 CDC Gun Mortality Data" (February 2021), p.6, accessed at http://efsgv.org/2019CDCdata

[9] CNN health, "Children and teens are more likely to die by gun than anything else" (March 2023), accessed at https://www.cnn.com/2023/03/29/health/us-children-gun-deaths-dg/index.html

[10] EVERYTOWN, "Firearm Suicides in the United States" (February 2023), accessed at https://everytownresearch.org/report/firearm-suicide-in-the-united-states/

[11] National Institute of Justice, "Public Mass Shootings" (February 2022), accessed at https://nij.ojp.gov/topics/articles/public-mass-shootings-data base-amasses-details-half-century-us-mass-shootings

¹² Sandy Hook Promise, " Say Something Creates Cultural Change That Leads To Safer Schools" (2022), accessed September 28, 2022, https://www.sandyhookpromise.org/our-programs/say-something/

¹³ Gallup, "What Percentage of Americans Own Guns?" (2020), accessed at https://news.gallup.com/poll/264932/percentage-americans-own-guns.aspx

¹⁴ Pew Research Center, "Key takeaways on Americans' views of guns and gun ownership." (June 2017), accessed at https://www.pewresearch.org/short-reads/2017/06/22/key-takeaways-on-americans-views-of-guns-and-gun-ownership

¹⁵The Trace, "How Many Guns Fall Out of Circulation Each Year In the U.S."" (October 2021), accessed at https://www.thetrace.org/2021/10/firearm-average-lifespan-how-many-lost-stolen-broken-guns

¹⁶ Bev Fitchett's Guns, "What Percentage of Crimes Are Committed With Stolen Guns?" (February 2023), accessed at https://www.bevfitchett.us/gun-laws/what-percentage-of-crimes-are-committed-with-stolen-guns.html

¹⁷ Pew Research Center, "What the data says about gun deaths in the U.S." (February 2022), accessed at https://www.pewresearch.org/fact-tank/2022/02/03/what-the-data-says-about-gun-deaths-in-the-u-s/

¹⁸ U.S. News, "U.S. Remains an Outlier in Firearm Possession, Gun-Related Deaths" (January 2023), C. Gilligan, accessed at https://www.usnews.com/news/best-countries/articles/2023-01-30/how-the-u-s-compares-to-the-world-on-guns

¹⁹ IBGVR Best Practices Guide, "Reporting on Community gun Violence? Here's What to do" (2022), accessed at https://ibgvr.org

²⁰ Forward Kentucky, "Five misconceptions about gun violence in the U.S." (December 2021), accessed at https://forwardky.com/five-misconceptions-about-gun-violence-in-the-u-s/

²¹ Alliance for Gun Responsibility, "Myth and Facts" (n.d.) accessed at https://gunresponsibility.org/myths-and-facts/

²² NiewmanReports, , K. Reed, "What Journalists Can Do To Report More Effectively-and compassionately-on Gun Violence" (November 2019), accessed at What Journalists Can Do To Report More Effectively — and Compassionately — on Gun Violence - Nieman Reports

²³BILLYPENNatWHYY, B. Seal, "Like I'm a nobody: Breaking news coverage of shootings is dehumanizing and delays progress, per Temple study" (January 2023), accessed at https://billypenn.com/2023/01/10/gun-violence-breaking-news-coverage-harmful-temple-study-jessica-beard/

²⁴ NiewmanReports, K. Reed, "What Journalists Can Do To Report More Effectively-and compassionately-on Gun Violence" (November 2019),

accessed at What Journalists Can Do To Report More Effectively — and Compassionately — on Gun Violence - Nieman Reports

[25] The Guardian, A. Clayton, "If I can hear you, I can find you" (June, 2019), accessed at 'If I can hear you, I can find you': the woman teaching kids to dodge bullets in their neighborhood | California | The Guardian

[26] Ibid.

[27] abcNEWS, "4-year-old accidentally shot, killed by younger sister in NW Harris County, according to HCSO" (March 2023), accessed at Child shot and killed by 3-year-old after gaining access to gun inside northwest Harris County apartment complex, HCSO says - ABC13 Houston

[28] NiewmanReports, K. Reed, "What Journalists Can Do To Report More Effectively-and compassionately-on Gun Violence" (November 2019), accessed at What Journalists Can Do To Report More Effectively — and Compassionately — on Gun Violence - Nieman Reports

[29] Ibid.

[30] N. Lee, P. Kotler, and J. Colehour, *Social Marketing: Behavior Change for Good,* 7th Ed. (Thousand Oaks, CA: SAGE, 2024), p.83.

[31] N. Lee, P. Kotler, and J. Colehour, *Social Marketing: Behavior Change for Good,* 7th Ed. (Thousand Oaks, CA: SAGE, 2024)

Chapter 22

Employers
Providing Workplace Safety Programs

Background

In November of 2022, a headline in an online news story stated: "Walmart shooting raises need for violence prevention at work."[1] The article went on to describe that a "31-year-old employee opened fire on fellow employees in the break room of the Chesapeake, Virginia, store, killing six people and leaving six others wounded. Police said he then killed himself." [2] It was stated to be one of the latest examples of a workplace shooting perpetrated by an employee.

The FBI defines incidents such as this one as an active shooter incident, one "when an individual is actively engaged in killing or attempting to kill people in a populated area through the use of firearms"[3], and that *over 80% of active shooter incidents happen at work.*"[4] The National Institute for Occupational Safety and Health identifies four categories for workplace violence: criminal intent such as robbery, customer/client conflicts, worker-on-worker, and personal relationships.[5] Additional data confirms reasons for concerns, and the need for interventions to reduce workplace gun violence:

- "In 2021, there were 387 cases of intentional workplace shootings resulting in the death of the victim."[6] This is similar to a 2018 report from the Bureau of Labor Statistics noting that in 2016 there were 394 workplace shootings that year resulting in death.[7] These annual stats equate to an average of 1 death per day in the U.S. from a workplace shooting.

- Data in 2022 indicated that only 45% of employees were aware of their company's violence prevention or safety plan.[8]
- "Homicide is the fifth-leading cause of workplace fatalities in the U.S., accounting for eight percent of all fatal on-the-job injuries."[9]
- One FBI study in 2015 reported that 51% of shooters in business environments were not employees or past employees of the business where the shooting took place; 47% were employed or previously employed by the business; and 2% were unknown.[10]

Strategies to reduce incidents of workplace gun violence noted by the National Safety Council include *policies* such as a zero-tolerance policy toward workplace violence and others related to access to guns at work locations; *technologies* at the worksite that provide weapon detection systems, panic buttons and cameras; and those focused on *employee safety programs* including trainings, knowing warning signs, active shooter simulations, and emergency action plans.[11] This chapter provides more detail on employee-focused programs, those illustrating a social marketing approach.

A Social Marketing Approach

Purpose & Focus

The social marketing approach presented in this chapter features efforts to *reduce gun deaths and injuries in the workplace* with a focus on *employers providing employee firearm safety programs*, preparing those in the workplace to react quickly to a potential or active shooter situation, lessening the impact.

Priority Audiences & Desired Behaviors & Insights

Employers have a variety of options for employee gun safety programs including trainings, live scenario simulations, and distribution of information regarding warning signs and escape protocols. Barriers, benefits, and motivators that *employers who don't currently offer formal programs to prevent or lessen the impact of active shooters* may have to providing these offerings include the following:

Barriers

- Beliefs that the policies they currently have provide enough protection, including a zero tolerance for workplace violence and required gun storage
- Low levels of concern that a shooting will happen at their worksite
- Costs for the trainings, including employee time spent
- Concern that employees will think they are at risk in the workplace, that maybe someone there is a potential shooter

Benefits

- Lessening the impact of an active shooter incident
- Saving lives, and avoiding injuries of employees
- Being viewed as a responsible employer

Motivators

- Potential liabilities for not offering programs include the requirement by the Occupational Safety and Health Act, which regulates workplace health and safety, that every employer provides employees with "a workplace free from recognized hazards that are causing (or are likely to cause) death or serious physical harm ... and employers found to be in violation may be cited by OSHA."[12]

- Potential monetary costs of injuries and deaths including workers' compensation benefits for injuries arising out of their employment,[13] as well as medical costs and potential lawsuits
- Availability of employee assistance programs that provide employees with resources
- Credible data regarding risks of gun violence in a workplace such as theirs
- Easy access to relevant and affordable employee safety programs

In is noted, of course, that *employees are the priority audience for the employers* and will guide the selection, as well as implementation, of program interventions. The importance of considering programs for all employees at the worksite is emphasized, given that anyone could play a vital role in lessening the impact of an active shooter incident.[14] "It's the employees who have their ear to the ground and know what's going on daily in the workplace with their colleagues."[15] And what employers will need to empower employees to do is to *be vigilant, report any concerns, follow protocols and access resources made available* to them.[16]

Key Strategies

Workplace Programs developed and offered by a variety of organizations including The Department of Homeland Security (DHS) support employees "to do" the following major actions to reduce the incidence and severity of workplace gun violence:

- *Recognize Warning Signs:* In the workplace setting, it would be ideal if employees reported to their manager or human resources department any "red flags" that may indicate a fellow employee may be at risk for committing acts of violence. Training programs would include more detail on what signs to look for among co-workers including violation of company policies, unexplained absenteeism, decline in job performance and depression.[17] Programs would also provide guidance on how and when to report these concerns.

- *React Quickly In An Active Shooter Situation:* Training programs provide detail on steps to take when a shooting is active in the workplace. DHS materials emphasize that because "active shooter situations are often over within 10 to 15 minutes, before law enforcement arrives on the scene", employees need to know how and when to take specific actions to evacuate, hide out, and, potentially, take action against the active shooter. [18]

- **STOP THE BLEED®:** As described in Chapter 8, DHS describes *Stop the Bleed* as a "national awareness campaign and call-to-action" and that it is critical since "a person who is bleeding can die from blood loss within five minutes. . . You may be able to save a life by taking these simple actions right after the trauma."[19] A downloadable poster with detailed graphics describes the 7 Steps to apply a tourniquet on the wound.

- *Respond When Law Enforcement Arrives:* DHS emphasizes that employees need to know that law enforcement's purpose is to stop the active shooter as soon as possible, and that they will likely first proceed to the area where shots were last heard. They will then offer treatment to injured persons and guide others to a safe location until the situation is under control.[20]

Tools

Formats for programs to provide and support recommended employee actions are varied and include:

- *Formal written plans* developed by the business, such as an Emergency Action Plan (EAP), will provide employees with policies for critical actions including reporting problems, gun storage, and escape routes in the case of a shooting.[21] Ideally, input is provided from several stakeholders including human resources, property managers, facility owners and local law enforcement.
- *Trainings* can be in person or online, and may be facilitated by a trained employee or an outside consultant. These are opportunities to support employee recognition of red flags, skills in "stopping the bleed", and understanding of where to go at the work location in the case of a shooting incident.
- *Simulations of an active shooter situation* is a mock event, one that employees are aware of ahead of time, and by implementing this "drill" employers can learn what responses are understood and where there may be need for improvement.
- *Manager and supervisor reinforcement* will be especially important in large workplace environments where situations may be varied and unique, such as regarding employees reporting on "red flags", and identifying escape routes.
- *Informational documents* can provide convenient and visible reminders of recommended employee actions such as an infographic for how to Stop the Bleed, posters noting exits to use in case of an active shooter, and a list of "red flags" to watch for in colleagues.

Access to Programs

Many program elements are available *online* such as the DHS's offering of a detailed downloadable booklet "ACTIVE SHOOTER: HOW TO RESPOND."[22] In addition, there are consultants who offer in person employee active shooter response trainings.[23]

Employee Communications

In addition to communications related to policies, trainings and internal documents, employers can help increase awareness, interest, and participation in these programs with additional tactics. Recommendations below include several, with specific action in italics from an NBC news article "How companies should deal with the threat of gun violence-and what employees can do":[24]

- Make your *gun policy at the workplace premise clear* to all employees
- Send a *personal handwritten letter* to employees and their families stating that management will do "everything we can" to create a safe workplace.
- Hold a *town hall meeting or breakfast* to engage employees in conversations about workplace safety and what programs are being developed and offered to employees to provide protection.
- Engage employees in *providing feedback* using instruments such as anonymous surveys asking questions to inform program enhancements. "Do you feel safe here at work? Are there other ideas you have for what we can do that would make it more likely you would report concerns about a colleague? Do you feel confident you would know how to respond to an active shooting incident?"

Applicable Behavior Change Theories

The *Health Belief Model*[25] is applicable for persuading employers to offer these programs. A review of the barriers including perceived costs of offering the programs (e.g., employee time spent) compared to the potential and desired benefits (e.g., saving lives) makes a case that employers could see that benefits outweigh costs.

The effectiveness and impact of employer workplace safety programs relies, in part, on recognition that these programs are to increase their employees' "Preparation" in the event of an incident, one described in the *Stages of Change Model*[26] as critical for advancing to "In Action."

Social Marketing Principles Contributing to Success[27]

Social marketing principles supportive of this case's approach include:

- Selecting *doable behaviors* with significant potential impact (e.g., know available exits and how to stop the bleed)
- Making *access easy* by providing employers with a variety of resources for trainings (e.g., Department of Homeland Security materials)
- Using *trusted messengers*, in this case citing FBI facts regarding incidents in the workplace and having immediate supervisors and managers reinforce validity and value of the safety programs

References

[1] abcNEWS, "Walmart shooting raises need for violence prevention at work" (November 2022), accessed at https://www.cbsnews.com/news/walmart-shooting-chesapeake-virginia-violence-prevention/

[2] Ibid.

[3] SHRM, "FBI: Over 80 Percent of Active Shooter Incidents Occur at Work" (March 2015), accessed at https://www.shrm.org/ResourcesAndTools/hr-topics/risk-management/Pages/FBI-Active-Shooter-Work.aspx

[4] Ibid.

[5] nscINJURY FACTS, "Assault at Work" (2023), accessed at https://www.nsc.org/workplace/safety-topics/workplace-violence.

[6] techjury, "15 Disturbing Workplace Violence Statistics for 2023" (February 2023), accessed at https://techjury.net/blog/workplace-violence-statistics/

[7] nbcNEWS, "How companies should deal with the threat of gun violence-and what employees can do", N. Spector, (April 2018), accessed at https://www.nbcnews.com/better/news/how-companies-should-address-gun-violence-what-employees-can-do-ncna862621

[8] techjury, "15 Disturbing Workplace Violence Statistics for 2023" (February 2023), accessed at https://techjury.net/blog/workplace-violence-statistics

[9] EHS Daily Advisor, M. Dean, "Guns at Work: Keeping Employees Safe in Troubling Times" (February 2022), accessed at https://ehsdailyadvisor.blr.com/2022/02/guns-at-work-keeping-employees-safe-in-troubling-times/

[10] SHRM, "FBI: Over 80 Percent of Active Shooter Incidents Occur at Work" (March 2015), accessed at https://www.shrm.org/ResourcesAndTools/hr-topics/risk-management/Pages/FBI-Active-Shooter-Work.aspx

[11] nscINJURY FACTS, "Assault at Work" (2023), accessed at https://www.nsc.org/workplace/safety-topics/workplace-violence

[12] EHS Daily Advisor, M. Dean, "Guns at Work: Keeping Employees Safe in Troubling Times" (February 2022), accessed at https://ehsdailyadvisor.blr.com/2022/02/guns-at-work-keeping-employees-safe-in-troubling-times/

[13] Ibid.

[14] hsi, "Corporate Active Shooter Response Training" (2023), accessed at https://hsi.com/solutions/active-shooter-training/corporations

[15] nbcNEWS, "How companies should deal with the threat of gun violence-and what employees can do", N. Spector, (April 2018), accessed at https://www.nbcnews.com/better/news/how-companies-should-address-gun-violence-what-employees-can-do-ncna862621

[16] Ibid.

[17] nscINJURY FACTS, "Assault at Work" (2023), accessed at https://injury facts.nsc.org/work/safety-topics/assault/

[18] U.S. Department of Homeland Security, "Active Shooter: How to Respond" (October 2008), accessed at https://www.dhs.gov/xlibrary/assets/active_shooter_booklet.pdf

[19] U.S. Department of Homeland Security, "Stop the Bleed" (October 2022), accessed at https://www.dhs.gov/stopthebleed

[20] U.S. Department of Homeland Security, "Active Shooter: How to Respond" (October 2008), accessed at https://www.dhs.gov/xlibrary/assets/active_shooter_booklet.pdf

[21] Ibid.

[22] Ibid.

[23] hsi, "Active Shooter Training-Empower Your Team" (2023), accessed at https://hsi.com/solutions/active-shooter-training

[24] nbcNEWS, "How companies should deal with the threat of gun violence-and what employees can do", N. Spector, (April 2018), accessed at https://www.nbcnews.com/better/news/how-companies-should-address-gun-violence-what-employees-can-do-ncna862621

[25] N. Lee, P. Kotler, and J. Colehour, *Social Marketing: Behavior Change for Good,* 7th Ed. (Thousand Oaks, CA: SAGE, 2024), pp.80-83.

[26] Ibid., pp.78-79.

[27] N. Lee, P. Kotler, and J. Colehour, *Social Marketing: Behavior Change for Good,* 7th Ed. (Thousand Oaks, CA: SAGE, 2024)

Chapter 23

Highlights of Case Examples In This Book
Facts, Audiences, Behaviors, Interventions,
Applicable Theories & Principles

Informative & Inspirational Facts

As noted in Chapter 1, the following facts inspired a focus for this book on Social Marketing approaches to reducing gun deaths and injuries from Suicides, Public Mass Shootings, School Shootings, Homicides, Gang-Related Shootings, and Domestic Violence. Examples of social marketing efforts to address these areas of focus led to featuring strategies to increase *Gun Storage, Reporting of Suspicious Activities, Protection from Domestic Violence, Reaching Out to Someone Who May Be Suicidal, Gang Crime Deterrence* and *Community Engagement.* The facts also made it clear that to maximize the impact of these efforts we need to use a *Social Equity* lens when developing program strategies.

Why gun deaths and injuries are a "public health" crisis, especially *Suicides*:

- 100+ Americans die every day, on average, from a gun injury (2015-2019).[1]
- More than 60% of gun deaths with intent are suicide, more than 65/day on average (2015-2019).[2]

- Gun injuries are the leading cause of death for children and teens since 2020.[3]
- 400+ Mass shootings occur every year, more than 1/day on average (2015-2019).[4]
- 50+ School shootings occur every year, almost 1/week on average (2015-2019).[5]
- 57 women are killed every month with a firearm by an intimate partner, almost 2/day on average (2022).[6]

Why gun *Storage* is a critical behavior to influence:

- 63% of gun owners have at least one gun in their home never locked up (2020).[7]
- Among children and youth under 18, over 80% of firearm suicides involved *a gun belonging to a family member.*[8]
- Almost *half of school shooters stole the gun from a family member.*[9]
- An estimated 300,000 guns are stolen each year from private owners, more than 800 a day (2020).[10]
- 96% of guns that are stolen are taken from private citizens (2017-2021).[11]
- Some studies have estimated that more than 80% of those arrested for a gun crime were armed with a stolen gun.[12]

Why *"Saying Something"* can help reduce gun deaths:

- Almost half of mass shooters "leaked their plan" in advance (2022).[13]
- For 4 out of 5 school shootings, at least one other person knew of the person's intent (2022).[14]

Why a *Social Equity* lens is important for program planners:

- 84% of gun homicide victims are Male (2019).[15]
- 53% of gun homicide victims are Black vs. 13% in the general population (2019).[16]

- Veterans represent almost 18% of gun suicide deaths even though they make up about 7% of the U.S. adult population.[17]

Major Audiences Prioritized

The following audience segments are ones noted as priorities for social marketing efforts featured in the case examples of this book. Within each of these prioritized segments, strategic emphasis was on *The Help Mes,* those who are open to "doing something" to reduce gun deaths and injuries:

- Gun owners with youth/children in the home who do not currently safely secure their guns
- Middle school, high school and college students who have a friend exhibiting signs they may be at risk for attempting suicide
- Friends, family members and colleagues of a Veteran who seems at risk for attempting suicide
- Pediatricians with patients 12 and older
- Middle & High School students, teachers, counselors, and parents
- School Threat Assessment Teams
- Youth and adults witnessing a mass shooting
- Attendees at large public events such as sports and entertainment venues
- Property managers
- Male high school youth who have carried a gun at least once in the previous 12 months, especially those who have experienced violence, suicidal ideation, or substance abuse
- Gang members at highest risk for gun violence offence
- Local neighborhood groups surrounding vacant lots
- Citizens living in neighborhoods at high risk for gun violence
- Street Outreach Workers
- Citizen Advocates for policy change

- Females experiencing domestic abuse
- Citizens who witness a suspicious gun violent activity
- Social Media groups who notice a warning sign of a potential gun violent activity
- Local police and public health agencies
- News Reporters & Journalists
- Employers of large workplace facilities

Major Behaviors Selected

As apparent in descriptions of case examples, this book focuses on **voluntary actions that citizens can take** to reduce gun deaths and injuries, versus laws and policies. The following protective and intervening actions are examples from cases presented in this book:

- Safely secure and/or store your guns.
- Reach out and have a conversation with a friend who seems at risk for attempting suicide.
- Pediatricians conduct universal screenings that will indicate risk for suicide.
- *Say Something* to a trusted source if you notice critical warning signs of potential gun violence.
- School Threat Assessment Teams assess reported threats of potential student acts of gun violence.
- Take an instructional *Stop The Bleed* course, similar to CPR for heart-related trauma.
- Administer *Stop the Bleed* procedures while waiting for professional help to arrive.
- *Know the Exits* when arrive at a public event.
- *Run. Hide. Fight.* in the case of a mass shooting at a public event.
- Reduce handgun carrying among at risk populations.
- Gang members accept an invitation to engage in group discussions for preventive actions.

- Accept violence prevention support services.
- Care for vacant lots and enhance street lighting in at risk neighborhoods.
- Intervene and support people in the community identified as having highest risk for gun violence.
- Influence elected officials to support measures that have strong public support.
- Download and utilize a recommended domestic abuse app.
- Report postings on social media that are high risk warning signs of potential gun violence.
- News reporters and journalists mention preventive actions that citizens can take to reduce gun deaths and injuries.
- News reporters and journalists provide timely and informative facts, when known, regarding gun violent acts (e.g., if the gun was stolen; whether someone knew in advance this might happen).
- Provide employee firearm safety programs in the workplace.

Major Marketing Interventions (4Ps) Employed

Examples of all four traditional marketing intervention tools were found in highlighted case examples.

Product Strategies (Tangible Goods & Services)

- Gun safes, trigger locks
- Apps to assist in talking to a friend who seems suicidal
- Suicidal screening platforms for pediatricians
- School safety lesson plans and curricula
- Anonymous reporting systems
- Workshops on being a trusted adult
- *Know the Signs* training programs
- *STOP THE BLEED* training programs
- School Threat Assessment Teams

- Designated shelters in event of a mass shooting
- Parent trainings
- Mentoring programs
- Group gatherings for gang members
- Support from social service agencies
- Counseling
- Instructional videos
- Vacant lots for Greening
- Enhanced street lighting
- Street outreach workers
- Mobile app for Domestic Violence
- Active shooter drills at workplaces
- School clubs
- Employee safety trainings

Price Strategies (Monetary & Nonmonetary Incentives & Disincentives**)**

- Free gun trigger locks
- Discounts on gun storage units
- Tax credits, rebates, exemptions from sales tax, and insurance incentives for gun safe or safety devices
- Free apps
- Anonymity for reporting suspicious acts
- Free toolkits
- Free trainings, workshops, courses
- Gun buyback programs offering gift cards
- Scholarships for students completing components of the *STOP THE BLEED* program
- Certificates of Completion for courses and trainings
- Cash stipends for greening vacant lots
- Pay for street outreach workers
- Visible acknowledgement of legislators successful in getting legislation passed in their state

- Featuring success stories of citizens reporting suspicious activities
- Free campaign materials for *See Something, Say Something*
- Pledges to protect children from gun violence

Place Strategies (Convenience of Access to Offerings)

- Toll free number to receive a free gun trigger lock
- Availability of gun locking devices at local police stations and special events
- Mobile apps easily downloadable
- Pediatrician access to screening tools on websites
- Online access to teacher training materials on school safety
- Law enforcement going to homes of at risk students to have discussion with parents
- Online sign up for *STOP THE BLEED* course
- Lectures for portions of *STOP THE BLEED* course available online
- Gang working groups meeting at a community facility, for ideal time of one hour
- Support services provided at community social service agencies
- Mobile Call-In Teams for gang violence intervention programs
- Home visits with parents of gang members
- Greening vacant lots located in neighborhoods with likely volunteers
- Enhanced lighting primarily in public housing developments with elevated crime rates
- Outreach workers walking around neighborhoods and interacting on streets
- Citizen advocates meeting in person with elected officials
- Social media group volunteer members offering to meet in person with person posting a warning sign

- Employee trainings in person or online

Promotions (Messages/Branding, Messengers, Communication Channels)

Messages and Branding:

- Safe Gun Storage Saves Lives
- Free Gun Trigger-Locks
- Start a Convo, Safe a Life
- See Something, Say Something
- Start With Hello
- STOP THE BLEED
- STOP THE BLEED Month
- Greening Vacant Lots
- Enhanced Street Lighting
- National Gun Violence Awareness Day
- National "If You See Something, Say Something" Awareness Day

Messengers:

- Friends
- Parents
- Neighbors
- School counselors
- Educators
- Local governmental agencies
- Community organizations
- Faith-based organizations
- Medical providers
- Community coalitions
- Street outreach workers
- Newscasters and journalists

Communication Channels:

- Websites
- Billboards
- Postcards
- Flyers and brochures
- Newsletters
- Phone calls
- Marches
- Postings on social media
- TV news
- Public Service Announcements
- Pocket cards
- Paid advertising: broadcast, social media, outdoor, print
- Posters in schools
- Signage in transit stations
- Special events
- Videos
- Blogs
- Presentations at community group gatherings
- In person interactions on streets in neighborhoods

Major Theories Represented

At the end of most chapters, it was noted what Social Marketing related theories were reflected in the development and/or implementation of case examples that were presented in that chapter.

Overall, the following theories seemed to be most "at play":

- *Building Social Norms:* Supporting the protective behavior to be seen as a *Social Norm*

- *Social Cognitive Theory:* Highlighting self-efficacy, as well as assurance that benefits from performing the behavior will outweigh costs
- *Health Belief Model:* Addressing audience perceptions of Susceptibility, Severity, Benefits, Barriers, and providing Cues to Action
- *Stages of Change:* Customizing strategies to move priority audiences from Precontemplation to Contemplation to Preparation to Action

Others noted to be relevant include:
- *Community Based Prevention Model:* Creating programs with support of community organizations and groups
- *Exchange Theory:* Increasing perceptions that desired benefits will be realized and that they will be equal to or greater than perceived costs associated with performing the behavior
- *Self-Efficacy:* Recognizing the audience will need to perceive they have the skills and knowledge to perform the behavior
- *Behavioral Economics Framework:* Creating tactics that acknowledge we do not always behave rationally and may need interventions to "nudge" our audience in the direction we want them to go (e.g., put desserts at the end of the lunch line)
- *Theory of Reasoned Action:* Emphasizing the need to move priority audiences from Awareness and Interest to Intention to Act

Major Social Marketing Principles Noted

Multiple principles for success were apparent in program and campaign examples presented. Those most frequently applied included ones to:

- Select and Support a *Single, Doable, Clear Behavior*

- Feature *Trusted & Influential Messengers*
- *Make Access Easy* to Obtain Products and Services as well to Perform the Desired Behavior
- Select a *Clear Priority Audience*
- *Gather Audience Insights* on Audience Barriers, Benefits, Motivators, and the Competition
- Offer a *Product* to Help Perform the Behavior
- Use As Many of the *4P Intervention Tools* As Needed to Remove Barriers, Provide Desired Benefits, Leverage Motivators and Outweigh the Competition
- Highlight Desired *Benefits* of Performing the Behavior
- Utilize *Points of Decision Making* for Communications
- Motivate Audiences with *Incentives*, both Monetary & Nonmonetary

Others noted include:

- Utilize a *Diversity, Equity, and Inclusion* Lens for Program Development and Implementation
- Highlight Costs of *Competing Behaviors*
- Take Advantage of Strategies and Learnings from *Prior and/or Existing Similar Campaigns*
- Incorporate Tactics to Make Performing the Behavior *Fun, Popular and Easy*

References

[1] EFSBV, "A Public Health Crisis Decades in the Making: A Review of 2019 CDC Gun Mortality Data" (February 2021), p.6, accessed at http://efsgv .org/2019CDCdata

[2] Ibid. p.7

[3] CNN health, "Children and teens are more likely to die by gun than anything else" (March 2023), accessed at   https://www.cnn.com/2023/03/29/health/ us-children-gun-deaths-dg/index.html

[4] CNN, "Mass Shootings in the US Fast Facts" (May 2023), accessed at https://www.cnn.com/2023/01/24/us/mass-shootings-fast-facts/index.html

[5] USA FACTS, "The latest government data on school shootings" (April 2023), accessed at   https://usafacts.org/articles/the-latest-government-data-on-school-shootings/

[6] CAP, "Guns and Violence Against Women" (January 2022), accessed at https://www.americanprogress.org/article/guns-and-violence-against-women/

[7] Reader's Digest, "Guns in America", (Nov. 2022), D. Saldana, accessed at https://www.rd.com/article/gun-violence-statistics/

[8] EVERYTOWN, "Firearm Suicides in the United States" (February 2023), accessed at https://everytownresearch.org/report/firearm-suicide-in-the-united-states/

[9] BROOKINGS, "School shootings: What we know about them, and what we can do to prevent them" (January 2022), R. Kowalski, accessed at https://www.brookings.edu/blog/brown-center-chalkboard/2022/01/26/ school-shootings-what-we-know-about-them-and-what-we-can-do-to-prevent-them/

[10] The Trace, "How Many Guns Fall Out of Circulation Each Year In the U.S."" (October 2021), accessed at https://www.thetrace.org/2021/10/firearm-average-lifespan-how-many-lost-stolen-broken-guns

[11] NFCTA, "PART V: Firearm Thefts" (January 2023), p.2, accessed at https://www.atf.gov/firearms/docs/report/nfcta-volume-ii-part-v-firearm-thefts/download

[12] Bev Fitchett's Guns, " What Percentage of Crimes Are Committed With Stolen Guns?" (June 2023), accessed at https://www.bevfitchett.us/gun-laws/what-percentage-of-crimes-are-committed-with-stolen-guns.html

[13] NIJ, "Public Mass Shootings: Database Amasses Detail of a Half Century of U.S. Mass Shootings with Firearms, Generating Psychosocial Histories" (February, 2022), accessed at https://nij.ojp.gov/topics/articles/public-mass-shootings-database-amasses-details-half-century-us-mass-shootings

[14] Sandy Hook Promise, " Say Something Creates Cultural Change That Leads To Safer Schools" (2022), accessed September 28, 2022, https://www.sandyhookpromise.org/our-programs/say-something/

[15] EFSBV, "Firearm Homicide" (February 2021), accessed at https://efsgv.org/learn/type-of-gun-violence/firearm-homicide/

[16] Ibid.

[17] BRADY, "Firearm Suicide Risk Among Veterans and Military Service Members" (2019), accessed at
https://americanaddictioncenters.org/veterans/suicide-among-veterans
https://www.bradyunited.org/fact-sheets/veterans-and-suicide